CALLED TO ACCOUNT

The story of one family's struggle to say no to abuse

M'Liss Switzer & Katherine Hale

The Seal Press

Dedicated to my husband
Chuck,
who denied himself and took up his cross

Cover design by Laurie Becharas.
Composition by The Typeworks, Vancouver, B.C.
Printed in the United States of America.
10 9 8 7 6 5 4 3 2 1

First Seal Press edition, September 1987.

Library of Congress Cataloging-in-Publication Data

Switzer, M'Liss.
     Called to account.
     1. Switzer, M'Liss.   2. Abused wives--United States--Biography.   3. Family violence--United States--Case studies.   I. Hale, Katherine.   II. Title.
HV6626.S95   1987   362.8'3 [B]   87-16675
ISBN 0-931188-55-5

Seal Press
P.O. Box 13
Seattle, Washington 98111

CALLED TO ACCOUNT

INTRODUCTION

The story you are about to read is true. However, I wish to emphasize to the reader that there were some unique circumstances which made our achievement in dealing with domestic violence in our family possible. To begin with, Minnesota is a forerunner in its domestic abuse program. Few states have the impartial laws, competent police enforcement, and cooperative judicial system that were made available to me when I called my husband to account for his abusive behavior.

Secondly, few states have the family-based domestic abuse counseling resources that we used. Included in one comprehensive program were individual therapy sessions, same sex counseling groups, couples therapy, children's groups and family sessions.

These two essential ingredients, the judicial system and the abuse-centered therapy sessions were absolutely necessary in assisting our family in the changes we made.

Called to Account has been written to demonstrate the importance of unbiased law enforcement systems in bringing abusers to account. It has been written to illustrate the effectiveness of a coordinated domestic abuse mental health program. I hope that the sharing of our story can lead to changes in the law in other places and the creation of adequate domestic abuse-centered therapy programs. The recycling of this unhealthy behavior can be stopped, but it will take a concerted community effort.

Most importantly, my desire is that *Called to Account* can provide hope for others who suffer from domestic violence by demonstrating our human potential to grow and change.

CHAPTER 1

It was cold and cloudy as I pulled up in front of the Edgecumbe Police Station. The building was old—a former elementary school—and was set back a good way from the street. Squad cars were neatly lined up in the parking lot, giving the station an appearance of authority and sobriety. The enormity of what I was about to do was heightened by the cold official look of the station, and my body shook not only from the chill of the afternoon air, but with inner fear and determination.

The snow along the curbs had been piled high earlier that day by the plows. I would have to climb over the banks of snow because so far, no one had come to clear the path by the street.

I got out of the car and picked my way toward the station, my low-topped boots filling with snow as I went.

Once inside the station I had no idea where to go. There were no receptionists, no officers, no signs to direct me. Only a long corridor with doors on each side. The hall was a dirty tan color, drab and uninviting.

As I was debating whether to go or stay, a door opened and a uniformed policeman stepped into the hall. He saw me and came rather hesitantly in my direction. His eyes seemed to be sort of naturally taking in everything about me—my size, my clothes, my manner.

"Can I help you?" he asked matter-of-factly.

I answered in a voice that was low and very quiet—it didn't sound like me at all. "Yes, please. Where do I go to file a charge?"

He looked bored. "What kind of charge?"

I hesitated. "My husband beat me up last night. I want to file a complaint against him."

A look of suspicion crept across his face. "What does he do that for?" he asked.

Tears sprang to my eyes. What difference did it make? If I knew that, I probably wouldn't be here. "Please, where do I go?" I asked again.

He shifted his weight from one foot to the other and yawned. "Well, right now is not a very good time. We're in the middle of changing shifts, so there's no one to help you for a while." He looked around him. "Plus," he added, "we're kind of rearranging the station furniture and everything is a little confused."

I could see that. But I said nothing, and waited.

"Why don't you come back later?" He finally suggested.

My heart fell to my shoes. I don't know what I had expected, but it wasn't this. For twenty years I had wished there was something I could do. I had thought about it, feared it, wanted it, debated the pros and cons. Now there was a law to help and I had to face an indifferent law officer. It had taken me twenty years to get here, and some unconcerned policeman wanted me to "come back later."

He must have read the look on my face. "In a couple of hours we ought to be able to help you," he said sympathetically.

I shook my head. "I can't. I'm on a pretty tight schedule—my children have to be picked up from school to go to music lessons, and then I have to make supper, and then my husband will be home." The words seemed to come out in a rush, as if I had to convince him.

4

"Well, then," he decided, "come back tomorrow." He looked at his watch, obviously tired of our conversation.

I pressed him further. "I can't," I said again. "My husband is off tomorrow and won't go back to work until Sunday."

"Okay," he said, as if it were all settled. "Come back Sunday."

It was a losing battle. I thanked him and turned to go, feeling the weight of defeat and disappointment overwhelming me. When would I find time and opportunity to come back?

As I walked away, the officer relented a little and called after me, "You could call Sunday, and we can send a squad car to take the report."

Just what I needed—to alert the neighbors and possibly Chuck to what I was doing. Without turning around and continuing toward the door, I shook my head. "Thank you, I'd rather see if I can come back another time."

As I left the station, I felt undone, unresolved, like I was left hanging in mid-air, at the mercy of gravity which was pulling me down. It was out of my control. *Come back later.* I couldn't believe I had just heard that. I was dumbfounded, full of misgiving. I wanted to stick my little finger in my ear and twist it to be sure I was still hearing okay. Yet, I was helpless to do anything else except to come back later if it were at all possible. The children would be waiting at school—I had to hurry. I started up the car and made my way across town, wiping the tears from my eyes as I went. I would have to get back to the station, but I couldn't imagine when I could possibly do it.

I spotted the kids immediately, even in the flow of students pouring from the building. Fourteen-year-old Rachel was surrounded by her friends, as usual, and I had to honk the horn to get her attention. Elgin, my ten-year-old son, came running to the car holding up his in-dex finger for me to see.

"Look, Mom," he shouted, "I hurt my finger in gym today, and I bet I can't play the cello at all."

"That's too bad," I sympathized. "How did you do it?"

They piled in the car and Elgin elaborated the details of his accident as we drove to their lesson. I only half listened, my mind in a whirl. Here was the extra time I needed to go back to the police station. Would things have improved there with the changing of shifts? And, what could I do with the kids?

Elgin and I waited while Rachel had her lesson. When we left I explained to the children that I had an errand to run, and that I would be dropping them off at Mac-Donalds for supper. They were delighted, and I gave Rachel some money and told her to wait at the restau-rant until I got back. About an hour, I thought.

For the second time that day, I headed for the police station. It was getting quite dark as I pulled up to the curb. The path to the door was illuminated by the fresh snow sparkling with the reflection from the street lights. As I walked in, I realized I still didn't know where to go. I stood for a moment, hesitant. When no one appeared after a few minutes, I walked down the corridor and opened the first door I found. The room was cluttered and disordered. There were boxes scattered everywhere and the furniture and desks were in random disarray. An officer was seated at a desk facing the door and I went over and stood in front of him.

"Where do I go to file a charge against my husband for beating me last night?" I asked, in a loud demanding voice. This time I would make them take me seriously.

The officer was instantly on his feet. He looked around as if hoping there would be someone else in the room. "Just a minute," he said, and left. A few minutes later, he was back with another officer trailing behind him.

"This is Sergeant Rickard," he said. "He's in charge of domestic abuse. He'll take your report."

The new officer looked at me and nodded. "Come this way, please."

I followed him down the corridor and into another classroom which was in much the same condition as the last one. We walked over to a desk in the middle of the room, which was surrounded by boxes, piled high. There were several other large desks scattered around, but these were unusable, stacked with more boxes and files.

He got me a chair and pulled it up to the desk, inviting me to sit down. "Sorry about the mess," he apologized. "I understand you want to file a complaint against your husband?"

"Yes, sir," I answered. "My name is M'Liss Switzer. My husband beat me up last night. I want the courts to force him to get some kind of treatment." I hurried on. "I understand there is now a law in Minnesota that allows the police to arrest for domestic abuse even if they don't see the incident. I want to file a charge against him and use that law to force him to get help."

He shifted in his chair and leaned back a little. "That's correct, but the arrest must be made within four hours of the incident."

My mind whirled at this new defeat. What should I do? Surely they didn't expect me to just wait for Chuck to beat me up again?

The sergeant noted my disheartened look and explained more clearly. "However, even though there can be no arrest in this situation, you can still file a charge and if there is sufficient evidence to prosecute, the city will proceed. Do you want to do that?"

I caught my breath. Here was new hope. "Yes, if I

could please," I answered.

He leaned forward and pulled some forms out of the drawer. "This won't take long Mrs. Switzer," he assured me. He picked up his pen and began to write. "Now let's get some specific information."

We went through the usual: name, address, place of employment, phone, etc. When he looked up at me again, he spoke softly, in a kind voice. "We'll need the details of the incident. Can you describe to me what happened?"

I took a deep breath and began. This was the part I had dreaded, but at least this officer seemed sympathetic, ready to listen and take me seriously. "My husband and I were driving to St. Mary's hospital to visit a friend last night. Chuck—my husband—was only vaguely familiar with the area and we soon got lost." I stopped, not sure how much to tell.

"Go on, please, Mrs. Switzer." he encouraged.

"Well, I knew where we were, but since he didn't ask me to advise him—sometimes that makes him mad—I didn't say anything. We drove around a few more minutes, then he shouted, 'We're going home—you didn't really want to go anyway.' On the way home, he got more and more excited, and he yelled at me, 'You knew where to go. Why didn't you tell me? You always seem to be there with the directions when I don't need them. What makes you so silent now? *You* think you're so smart, don't you!'" My voice broke, and I stopped for a minute. Sergeant Rickard waited, and I sensed his understanding and patience.

"That's when he started hitting me," I said, more quietly.

Sergeant Rickard interrupted. "How, Mrs. Switzer? How did he hit you? Can you show me how he did it?"

I demonstrated. "He hit me with his fist, like this." I closed my right hand into a fist and swung it from my left shoulder, across in front of me, and out to my right side, as if I were trying to hit someone to the right of me. "He hit me across the chest and shoulders over and over — a lot of times. I put up my arm to protect my chest."

Sergeant Rickard nodded. "Good. And then what happened?"

I thought, then continued. "Well, Chuck had to stop for a red light, so I tried to open the door and get out of the car. But it didn't work. Chuck reached across me and locked my door. He grabbed my seat belt and pulled it across my neck and chest and held it there until we got home. He kept yelling at me and criticizing me while he was drivng. But by the time he let me out of the car, he had calmed down. That's all."

When I finished, he leaned forward and looked at me directly. "Mrs. Switzer," he asked, "do you have any marks or bruises from the incident to support your story?"

I had expected the question, and it wasn't asked unkindly. "Yes, I was wearing a heavy down jacket, but I still have some bruises on my shoulder."

He nodded again. "When you get home," he advised, "have someone take a picture of your shoulder as soon as possible. You'll need it as evidence if the city should decide to take your case. He paused and then continued, "Are you sure he hit you with his fist, and not just an open hand?"

"Yes," I reassured him, shaking my head in the affirmative, "I'm sure."

"Very good. Your report will be investigated. It will take about three weeks to determine whether or not we will take your case. As part of our investigation, we'll need some other information." The sergeant continued. "Has this kind of thing ever happened before?"

"Yes," I answered steadily. "It's been going on for the past twenty years." I almost felt him flinch, but outwardly he remained unchanged.

Looking up from his paper, he inquired, "Have you

ever seen a doctor as a result of injuries from the abuse?"

Again, I had thought this through, and I was prepared. "Yes—two different times. But I was too embarrassed to tell the doctors what had really happened —I just made up a story."

"That doesn't matter. We'll still need their names and permission for access to your medical records." He handed me a medical release form and a pen.

"There's one more thing," I added. "A few years ago —ten years after our marriage, Chuck agreed to see a psychiatrist for a while. I went with him for the first several weeks, and he continued on by himself for a number of years. It didn't do much good, but the records might help document the problem."

"Good," he said, sliding another medical release form toward me. "We'll need that too."

For the next few minutes, the officer continued to question me about past incidents; when they occurred, how violent they had been, if the children or anyone else had witnessed any of the encounters. I told him that to my knowledge, only the children had ever seen the abuse.

After taking down this information, he rose to indicate the interview was over. "Mrs. Switzer, I believe I have all the information we need to do a preliminary investigation—you'll just need to get that photograph to me right away."

I nodded.

"After that," he went on, "it will take about three weeks to determine whether or not the city will prosecute. And if they do, a court date will be set, and your husband will be summoned to appear."

I waited, then asked the obvious question. "And if they choose not to prosecute?"

"The case will be dropped." His voice trailed off.

"Then what would I do?" I pressed on, not wanting to hear what I knew the response would be.

The officer didn't want to give the answer any more than I wanted to hear it. He hesitated several seconds before replying, "Wait until it happens again, and then repeat this procedure. But," he added, "next time we'll already have this report to support your case."

I sensed he was trying to encourage me, so I thanked him and let him escort me to the door. "Just one more thing, Officer," I stopped to face him. "If the city does decide to prosecute, will I be notified before they tell Chuck?"

He realized immediately the importance of his answer. "I'll see to it, Mrs. Switzer, that you're notified in advance if your husband is to receive a summons."

As I walked out into the cold night air, I felt a ton of weight being lifted from my shoulders. I realized at that moment I would have never made it back to the station if I had had to wait until Sunday. It was today, or not at all.

I took a deep breath and let the tears flow down my cheeks. The cold of the winter night froze them quickly on my face, and I remembered another time I had felt cold, and alone, and desperate.

CHAPTER 2

It had been snowing then too. I was twelve years old at the time. I was out shoveling in front of our house and as I shoveled, I noticed a car pull up in front of the house next door, my father's house. I saw a man get out and walk up to his door. I kept shoveling. In a moment, the man came over and stopped right in front of me.

"I've been knocking on the door of that house," he said, pointing in the direction of my father's house, "and no one answers. I'm Mr. Bock's insurance agent, and I need to get in touch with Mrs. Bock. Do you know where she is?"

I paused, momentarily confused since my mother had been Mrs. Bock at one time. At this point they had been divorced eleven years. They both had remarried two years before, but the names were often a problem for me. My last name remained Bock, but my mother's had changed to Collett. Assuming he wanted my father's third wife, I finally answered, "No, I'm sorry, I don't know."

With a look of defeat, he turned slowly around and headed for his car. "Well, thanks anyway." Then he paused in his tracks and turning back towards me, added as an afterthought, "He died yesterday, you know?" Without waiting for a reply, he shrugged his shoulders and walked away.

I stood there stunned, my mouth hanging open in disbelief. I watched him get into his car and pull away. It couldn't be true. Someone would have told me. I threw down my shovel and ran towards my house. I scurried through the front door and up the stairs, taking them two at a time until I reached the top. Bursting into my mother's room, I cried, "Mother, Daddy's dead, Daddy's dead." "Please," I begged her silently, "say it isn't true."

My mother had been bedfast for months suffering with cancer. Now as I approached her bed, a look of pain and deep sorrow crept across her face. Finally she spoke, "Yes, I know."

My oldest sister was in charge of the house since Mother was sick, and now she came up to me from somewhere there in the room. Taking me by my arm without a word, she ushered me out. I turned pleadingly toward my mother as we left. Her eyes were full of tears. Her brow was wrinkled, and her face held a look of despair and agony.

"Why didn't anyone tell me?" I pleaded with my sister when we were out in the hall and the door was closed.

She continued to lead me away and down the stairs. "Mother was shocked and upset by the news. We were afraid if you knew it, you would upset her more." She looked at me sternly. "Don't bring the subject up around her again, do you understand?"

Not understanding at all, but afraid of my sister who was nine years older and very strict with me, I nodded, "Yes."

She escorted me to the front door, and opened it. "Now go and finish shoveling."

I stopped in the doorway, still stunned and bewildered. "But, how did he die?"

She slowly started closing the door to keep out the cold as I stepped backwards onto the porch to get out of the way. "He had a heart attack in his store yesterday afternoon and he died shortly after, before the ambulance arrived." There was a pause, and the door clicked shut.

I stood for a moment looking at the blank hard wood that separated me from my sister. Then I turned and went back to the sidewalk. As I bent over to pick up my shovel, which still lay in the snow where I had left it, the tears streamed down my cheeks and quickly turned to ice.

The funeral was the following day. It had been decided for me that it would be best if I didn't go. No more was said, and that was all I was told.

Meanwhile, my mother's condition continued to deteriorate. In less than a week after my father's funeral, my mother began to hemorrhage.

I was lying on the living room floor doing my homework when I heard her scream out. I tore up the stairs and when I reached the top, my heart fell to my toes. My aunt and oldest sister were frantically running back and forth from my mother's room to the bathroom, carrying blood-soaked towels and bringing back dry ones. My sister ran past me, a towel of blood dripping in her hands. She called to me over her shoulder, "Quickly, have someone call an ambulance."

I flew down the stairs in a panic. My sister's husband was by this time standing at the bottom. "Call an ambulance, hurry," I cried out, "call an ambulance!"

I stayed downstairs pacing the floor and waiting for help to arrive. When I heard the siren, I ran to the door and held it open for the men unloading the stretcher. As they hurried through the door, I directed them past me and up the stairs. I watched as they manipulated the stretcher around the corner of the landing and on up to the second floor.

"We'll have trouble with that corner coming down." I heard one of them say.

A few minutes later I heard my mother cry in pain as

they lifted her from the bed onto the stretcher. I hurried to the bottom of the stairs wringing my hands in fear as they began their descent.

"We'll have to lift her over the banister to make that corner," one of the attendants remarked. With every downward movement, she groaned in pain. Then came the landing and the maneuver of lifting her over the banister. As they did, she screamed out in anguish. I leaned forward to see better, but otherwise didn't move as they continued at a snail's pace to gently guide her down. When they reached the main floor, I couldn't stand back any longer. I bolted forward to her side, crying in terror, "Mother, Mother!"

She turned to look briefly at me, her face tortured. My oldest sister grabbed me by my shoulders and pulled me back. The attendants moved my mother away and out the door. That was the last time I saw her alive. She died the following Saturday. She had taken a turn for the worse on Friday night and the hospital called early Saturday morning to say she was dying. My oldest sister and her husband, along with my aunt and stepfather all left immediately to be with her. I and my other sister Dorothy, who was two years older than I, were left alone in the house to wait.

It seemed like an eternity. As soon as we heard them pull up in front, we ran to the door, not knowing what to expect. Yet, we knew immediately from the look of sadness on their faces that our mother was dead.

I started to cry softly, but the true reality of what had happened and what I had lost was beyond my grasp. The days that followed were a blur; the planning of the funeral, the arrangements with the minister, the gathering of her things for the mortician, the two days of visitation at the funeral home—it all ran together, like dark colors in the wash.

Before I could comprehend all that was happening, the day of the funeral had arrived, and I found myself standing with my two sisters and my stepfather beside my mother's gray-trimmed casket. Her face was pale against her dark dress and someone had pinned a soft pink carnation to her shoulder, giving her a little color. As she silently lay there, I began to sense the gulf that separated us. The funeral director reverently stepped forward and began closing the casket. As I watched the lid descending over her peaceful face, I realized I was seeing her for the last time; that she was dead. Feeling orphaned, a vacuum of emptiness engulfed me. I felt hopelessly alone, deserted to survive on my own. I began crying, softly at first, but then, like waves surging upon the shore, my grief rushed in on me with stronger and stronger force, until I was sobbing uncontrollably. I was alone. My mother was gone forever.

My oldest sister took me by the arm and led me out of the chapel to the drinking fountain, urging me as we went, "Get control of yourself and stop this crying. You're making a scene."

My head jerked with my sobs as we approached the fountain. She held the faucet as I bent to drink, rubbing my back as I sobbed and gasped. I came up for air, still jerking, my chest heaving with my sorrow. "She's gone," I cried, "I'll never see her again."

With helplessness and impatience in her voice, my sister answered. "M'Liss, stop it. You're upsetting Grandpa, and if you keep on like this, he'll break down."

Sensing the tenseness in her voice, and fearing her anger, I bent over the fountain and took another drink. I raised back up, still shuddering as I whispered, "I think I'll be okay."

Sounding less irritable, she encouraged me with "You're all right, M'Liss, you can do it." She handed me another kleenex and led the way back to the chapel where the service was about to begin.

And that was that—my moment of consoling comfort, my moment of reassurance that I would be "okay." I felt desolate and apart, with no one to care for me, and a long way to go.

With my father and mother gone, the responsibility for Dorothy and me fell upon my oldest sister. She and her husband moved in, and she became our legal guardian. Things ran smoothly at first, but the novelty of two teenage girls to raise soon wore thin. Though we were old enough to take care of ourselves, there were still added work and obligations for her. She went from cleaning a modern two-room apartment to an old three-story house; from washing for two to washing for four; from cooking for two to cooking for four. As time went by, she became resentful and angry. Her only consolation was the Social Security check she received once a month from the government. Her anger began manifesting itself. It would come out in the things she would say to me and the foul language she would use. It would come out in the way she treated me, not just by how and what she said, but with physical abuse as well. I became the scapegoat for her anger, though Dorothy wasn't neglected. I never knew what could set her off. I tried to stay out of her way as much as possible. She was extremely moody and she drank. On Saturdays I would get up early and do my chores as quickly and quietly as I could so I would be out of there before she got up. She hated getting up in the morning and I could always count on her being crabby when she did. After a cup of coffee and a cigarette, she was better, if I could just stay away until then.

She allowed no room for errors. If I failed to do a task properly, to her specifications, I wasn't allowed to do it again. I learned this not long after Mother's death when my sister told me to make a cake. I mixed it all up, greased the pan, and put it in the oven. When the time was almost up for the cake to be done, I smelled something burning. I pulled out the cake and found that on one end of the loaf pan it was thin and burned, and on the other end it was thick and raw. My oldest sister was smelling the smoke by this time and came rushing into the kitchen demanding to know what was going on. I showed her the cake. She was furious. She looked in the oven and found the shelf was in wrong. The back of the shelf was up on a higher rung than the front, causing the cake batter to run forward in the pan. She started yelling, calling me a "God-damned stupid idiot" for not having checked the shelf before I put the cake in. Then she took the pan and threw it across the room. As she went into the storeroom she continued berating me, telling me how wasteful and careless I was. She came out swinging a broom, hitting me several times. When she was through, she flung it down and told me to clean up my mess.

After that, she never let me bake again and she began treating me as though I was too stupid to do anything important. Whenever we had company and the fine china dishes were used, she wouldn't let me help with the clean-up because I "would probably break something." She would always make a point of this in front of the guests, humiliating me. I didn't mind getting out of the dishes for a change, but my feelings were hurt and my self-worth diminished by her unkindness.

It was the same thing when it came to doing the ironing. She said I was unteachable and too careless to iron. She was sure I would scorch something. So she hired one of my girlfriends to do it. That added insult to injury. My friend asked me why I didn't do it but I was too embarrassed to tell her. My sister would give my friend ten cents for each piece she did, and then gripe at me for having to pay it. She resented being out the money and me "getting out of work." She would tell me, "You're not worth shit, because if you were, I wouldn't have to hire someone to do your work." Yet she never gave me the chance to even try.

I got the same message when I was old enough to learn to drive. She refused to allow her husband to teach me because in her words, I was "too God-damned irresponsible to be trusted with the car."

When my sister and her husband bought a lake home, she wouldn't take me to see it or even tell me where it was. She said if I knew I would probably sneak up there with some of my friends and have a wild party. I didn't have any wild friends and I would never have even considered doing such a thing anyway. That insult cut deep. I felt in a quandary, bewildered, confused. Why did she think I was so bad? I felt falsely charged, accused of indiscretion, indicted as disrespectful of others' property.

She didn't like the way I looked either. She often told me I was too big-busted. When I wore a sweater, she said I was immodest, a "God-damned cheap slut." She told me I was ugly, that no one would ever marry me and that she would have me on her hands the rest of my "God-damned life." I believed her prediction could come true. I was cross-eyed and wore thick glasses. My teeth were very crooked, and I had worn braces for years. In general, I felt conspicuous and repulsive, unlovable and unloved.

Though her husband was never abusive physically or verbally, he never intervened except once. I had failed to mash the potatoes to her satisfaction. Taking the masher from me, she beat me over the head with it, calling me a "God-damned lazy shit." As I ran from the room, I could feel a warm trickle on the back of my neck. I went over to my brother-in-law, who was reading the paper and asked him to check my head. He saw that it had been cut and gave me his handkerchief. Then he got up and went into the kitchen. I heard him ask my sister if she didn't think she had gone too far, since my head was bleeding.

Her response was, "Mind your own God-damned business." He didn't press the issue further, but returned to the living room and told me to go put some ice on my head. I went reluctantly, afraid of my sister who was still in the kitchen. She was getting some ice from the freezer, but as soon as she saw me, she got mad all over again and threw it at me. Next came a package of frozen weiners, aimed at my head. I retreated from the room quickly, grabbing some ice up off the floor as I went.

When my sister and her husband fought with each other, I was terrified. What if they would divorce? Then what would happen to me? Their fights were loud and she would go storming upstairs slamming doors as she went. At those times, I was especially careful to stay out of her way. I felt so unprotected, helpless and insecure.

When I considered getting a part-time job in my last years of school, I was met with mockery. "Who would hire you?" My first application ended in rejection. They weren't hiring just then. For that I got: "Ha, ha, I told you so." It was a whole year before I tried again. I got a job working in a dime store. The sarcastic conclusion for that was: "That's all you're good for. That's the best you'll ever do."

She constantly told me I was too dumb to graduate from high school. When I did graduate, she said they must have lowered their standards since she went to school.

After graduation, I worked for an airline. The company provided me with two free passes a year to fly anywhere in the continental U.S. I wasn't allowed to use them. The excuse: "You can't be trusted." What I ever did to show I was untrustworthy I'll never know. I didn't smoke, drink, swear; I went to church every week, taught Sunday school and sang in the choir. I didn't date boys, I was too homely. I felt defeated.

When I would share with my girlfriends or their parents the treatment I was receiving at home, they were sympathetic, but there was nothing they could do. It really wasn't their business. They didn't want to get involved. If I mentioned it to anyone from church, I was met with disbelief. After all, my sister had taken me in, hadn't she? How could she turn around and do a thing like that? So, I began to believe *I'm not okay*. And to spare myself further humiliation, I learned to keep it to myself. My sister never admitted being wrong, or sorry. My thinking took on the form of, *It must be okay. This is the way people are.*

The thought of leaving home did not occur to me. I was convinced I couldn't handle life on my own. Plus, I owned a third of the house, so how could I leave? I did mention moving out on one occasion when I was feeling especially confident and daring. I was met with, "Well, you ungrateful, God-damned good-for-nothing." And, the big hooker, "You will upset Grandpa if you move out." Grandpa lived two doors away. I was still being controlled by messages concerning the needs of others over my own needs.

After I had worked for three years, I decided to go to college. The gibes I took for that did not discourage me. I loved it. I even made good grades. And then, a wonderful thing happened to me.

CHAPTER 3

I was sitting in the college study hall one morning before class when a handsome young man in horn-rimmed glasses and a light blue ski sweater walked up and asked if he could sit next to me. After all my past programming about being ugly, I was really surprised. I managed to stammer out a reply, and we began to get acquainted. Our courtship lasted a year and two months before we were married.

Chuck became familiar with my situation at home and urged me to leave. With his encouragement and help, I found an apartment and moved out. It was so simple, yet without his support and advice, I wouldn't have dared risk such a step on my own. I lacked the confidence to believe I could handle the responsibility of taking care of myself, and I feared my sister's reaction if I stood against her. Chuck's encouragement and support was all I needed to take that step. He had challenged my erroneous impression—the belief that I couldn't leave, that I couldn't manage. He helped me realize that my sister had no hold on me, that I was legally and physically free to leave anytime I chose. Because of his influence and support my sister did not like or approve of him. She considered him incompetent, unskilled, ignorant, "someone who would never amount to anything."

Chuck came from a background similar to mine. Perhaps that was one of the things that attracted us to each other. But while I had seen no escape from my situation, he couldn't leave home soon enough. Chuck's move north to go to college was a form of retreat for him. He hated his home and parents. He had been physically abused so badly as a child, it made my abuse look enviable. Chuck didn't hear the foul language I did, nor did he receive the same obvious "put downs," but he was quelled in other ways.

His parents ran a dairy farm, but his father worked in town. The heavy responsibilities of milking and plowing fell on his mother and at an early age on him. His mother was over-burdened with the tremendous load of farming, housekeeping, cooking, raising four children— one year apart each—no running water, no electricity, etc. The pressures were too great and she took it out on Chuck and his sisters and brother. His mother's abuse against him took on the form of beatings from an irrational state of mind. The beatings would be far more savage than the infraction warranted.

On one occasion, when Chuck neglected to accomplish some task he had been assigned, she became enraged and expressed that fury by dragging him to the milk cooling trough and holding him down under the water shouting, "I'm going to kill you!" On another occasion, when she was annoyed with him, she tried to run him down with the tractor, conveying the same message as she chased him around the field.

When Chuck was thirteen years old, he began to hit back. This was something I would never have dared to do. It happened one day when he was out working in the field. He heard his sisters and brother screaming and crying from the house. Above their din came the shrill shrieks of his mother. Chuck ran from the field to help them. When he got to the house and tried to stop her, she picked up a baton and began beating him. In that moment, Chuck began to hit back. With his hands clenched into fists he charged into her, hitting at her face, chest, and stomach. Exhausted at last, she fell to the ground, murmuring she was too tired to go on.

After that, it became the norm. She would get angry and take a swing at him and he would raise his arm in self-defense and then haul off and let her have it either with a shove, or a hit. This became a frequent occurrence.

The worst battle that transpired between them happened when Chuck was about seventeen. He was alone with her in the car. Feeling cold, he reached over and turned the heater on. She was instantly irritated, snapping as she reached out to strike him with her arm, "You ask permission before you do that." Her arm struck him squarely in the face, causing his nose to bleed profusely. He began hitting her back while at the same time blowing the blood from his nose all over her coat. She continued slapping him and between their struggle and her trying to drive, the car ran into the ditch. That didn't stop them. The fight went on until they were too exhausted to continue. She got out of the car and walked home. Chuck, after catching his breath, backed the car out of the ditch and drove home.

His dad's abuse took on a different form. He beat Chuck too, but he also carried on a more subtle battle, one of the mind. He subverted Chuck with criticism and disapproval, destroying his self confidence and self-worth.

Whenever Chuck milked the cows, his father would take exception to the way he did it, chiding that he didn't squeeze all the milk out. Or he'd frown on the way Chuck cleaned the stalls. Or he'd reproach him for the way he fed the cows. Or he'd criticize him for not plowing the fields straight enough. Chuck rarely heard "good job." It was always "You could have done it better, you should have done it faster, why didn't you do it this way, or that way." When he worked in the garden, his dad would come along and berate him for being slow or for not being thorough enough. Chuck began feeling useless, unfit, unproductive, helpless. He wanted to get back at his dad, he felt rebellious and revengeful.

Whenever he had an idea to share, his dad nullified it by saying something negative. Then Chuck would feel foolish for having made the suggestion in the first place. When his dad tried to help him with his reading, it ended up in ridicule and mockery.

When he was told to haul in firewood with the tractor and wagon, and found the tires flat, he was accused of letting the air out. If the tractor wouldn't start, he was charged with intentionally sabotaging it so it wouldn't go. He felt incriminated as untrustworthy, indicted as sneaky, his self-trust slowly undermined.

The worst beating Chuck ever received from his dad happened when he was about six years old. There was a bully at school who kept picking on him, as well as the other boys and girls. One night, when Chuck's mother left her wedding rings on the sink, Chuck found them. He decided to take them to school and give them to the bully as a bribe to get him to leave Chuck and the others alone. When the bully arrived home, his folks wanted to know where he had gotten the rings. After he told them, they called Chuck's folks and informed them that Chuck had given the rings to their son.

In the meantime, Chuck's mother had been searching frantically and asking the children if any of them had seen her rings. Of course, Chuck lied and said he didn't know anything about them. When his dad found out what he had done, and that he had lied, Chuck was told that his punishment would be a spanking with the paddle for ten minutes.

During the first five minutes, Chuck began to lose control of his bowels. He hollered and yelled that he needed to go to the bathroom. When his dad finally let him, he couldn't go. He then returned for the last five minutes of the beating. In the meantime, his dad had rested, so, when Chuck returned, he was thwacked with renewed force. He had open blisters on his buttocks and he couldn't sit down for two weeks. After that, when his mother threatened him with "Wait until your dad gets home," he waited in terror and anticipation. He had learned what it was to "have the shit beaten out of him" and "not sit down for a week." His relationship with his dad became one of fear and dread for the unmerciful, unrelenting, taskmaster who seemed to have no understanding, tolerance or appreciation for what he did.

The most insensitive and heartless thing Chuck's dad did to him happened when he was nine. He shared a pet dog with his younger brother who was five. It was their responsibility to feed and water it. They forgot from time to time and the dog got hungry and started killing the chickens. Consequently, the dog had to be killed. So their dad took both boys outside and before their young eyes beat the dog to death with a hammer and made them haul it away. As a result of that incident, Chuck became apathetic and cold as far as his relationship with his dad was concerned. He became calloused and disrespectful. He hated him.

On another occasion, Chuck asked his dad if a certain light socket was working and his dad told him to put his finger in it. Unsuspecting, he did, only to receive a shock. His dad sat laughing while Chuck hardened his heart still more against him.

If his dad was missing a tool or part, he would accuse Chuck of taking it. If Chuck denied it, then he and his sisters and brother would be assigned the task of looking for it until it was found. In the meantime, his dad would occasionally taunt him with "Can't remember what you did with it, can you?" or "Don't have a very good memory do you?" This search process could go on through mealtime and up until it was too dark to continue. This "missing, accuse, and hunt game," would happen often enough that Chuck soon realized it was sometimes just a setup to keep him and the others out of his dad's hair. His resentment grew.

The most dramatic instance between Chuck and his dad took place when he was eighteen. He was assigned the task of digging a hole in solid clay stone with two other fellows who were working for his dad at the time. They were to dig it with pick and shovel, though it should have been dynamited. They worked for five hours in the hot, dry, July sun and made little progress. When his dad finally came along to view their advancement, he took one look and was instantly furious. Chuck could see it in the look on his face. The muscles were tight, his brow wrinkled, but his comment was cool and calculated. "Is that all you've done?" He took the pick ax and began himself to whale away at the clay and stones, like a mad man. As he did, he ridiculed them with accusations, stating that they were slow and incompetent, that they should have done better, done more, done it like he was doing it, and asking what was wrong with them that they couldn't do it as well as he could.

One of the fellows looked at him in exhausted disgust and told him he wanted a different job. So he left. Chuck was filled with rage. He felt powerless to stop him, tired and humiliated. He made up his mind, that if his dad uttered just one more word, he would kill him. He grasped the handle of his pick ax and raised it slightly, ready at the next word to hit him in the back. The message he was hearing again was that he could never do anything right, or good enough. He felt defeated, incapable of accomplishing anything to his dad's satisfaction.

So Chuck was victimized, by physical as well as emotional abuse. In addition, he witnessed his father and mother in physical combat with each other. His earliest childhood memory is that of seeing his parents involved in a physical fight. They were actually rolling on the ground in a skirmish. On one occasion, his father would attack his mother, on another, it would be vice versa. From Chuck's perspective, their fighting was an ongoing affair, with both physical and verbal abuse. It never seemed to end. One battle would only lead to another. It felt like there was no intermission. Hitting, fighting, beating must be okay. After all, his parents did it. And when he would go to school bruised and beaten, the teachers would inquire what had happened, but they did nothing about it. They remained uninvolved. Society was indifferent. No one ever said it was wrong. No one ever interfered. No one said they were sorry. Violence and abuse must be the way to deal with anger, it must be okay.

CHAPTER 4

Chuck and I went together for a year. During this time, he lived in the school dorm and later in an apartment. Our dating consisted of picnics, bike rides, long walks, movies, and friendly chats as we got acquainted, finding out what each other was like.

Away from his folks and from the pressures of home, Chuck decided that college was not for him. He dropped out of school in the third quarter and took a truck-loading job at a department store. Near the end of summer, he joined the Marine Corps and we set our wedding date for December after he completed his basic training. From boot camp, he would be assigned a new duty station. He arranged to go to his newly assigned station after our wedding, using his travel time for our honeymoon.

Like all wedding days, ours was filled with tension and excitement, last minute deadlines and arrangements. Nevertheless, everything went off as planned: the wedding, the reception, pictures, good byes. We were packed up and ready to go by six-thirty that night. I had rented a U Haul trailer, and we had spent the morning before the wedding packing all our belongings in it. After the reception, we added our gifts, filling not only the remainder of the trailer, but the back seat of our little Volkswagon Beetle.

Chuck's next assigned duty station was to be Millington, Tennessee. We had two weeks to get there, so we took off, heading south from St. Paul, Minnesota.

We made it as far as Des Moines, Iowa, arriving about ten that night. We found a little motel on the outside of town, just north of the city, and pulled in. Our car was all decorated up with crepe paper streamers, and lettering in white shoe polish with words like "better luck next time, just married, fools," etc. We stuck out as newlyweds like a piece of coal in a snow drift.

The small lobby was decorated in Christmas garb; a tree in the corner, ornaments and boughs around the doors, mistletoe over the counter (you were supposed to kiss the clerk). At the registration desk, the clerk stood grinning sheepishly at us. He had seen us pull up and had recognized our newlywed state.

"Just married, hah, well, I don't need this mistletoe for a kiss," he said as he leaned over the counter and gently kissed me on the cheek. "It's pretty quiet this time of year, so if you're looking for a room, I'll give you our bridal suite at no extra charge," he continued.

Chuck, who had been wanting to wash off the car even before we left St. Paul, was suddenly glad to have the advertisement. "That would be really nice of you," he replied, as he picked up a pen and started filling out the registration form.

"Think nothing of it. It's the season of giving and I'm glad to oblige," he said, handing Chuck the key. "Just drive down to the end of the building. It's the last door on the left."

"Thanks again," said Chuck, pocketing the key and taking my hand.

"Have a pleasant evening," the clerk replied in jest. "Check out time is eleven-thirty."

The door fell shut behind us as we got back into our car and headed down the lot to the end room. We parked diagonally so that the trailer wouldn't block anyone's way.

Chuck came around and opened my door, grabbing our bags from the back seat. He unlocked the door and we stepped into a pleasant room with two double beds, a settee, a dressing table and a large double-sink bathroom. The carpet was a soft pink, and the drapes and bedspreads were of a large flowered print. The settee was upholstered in soft matching pink colors with a little reading light and table beside it.

"Oh, how pleasant," I exclaimed in delight, adding in merriment, "and we each get our own bed."

"Why do you suppose they have two beds in a bridal suite?" Chuck asked in innocent wonder.

"I suppose they use this room as a regular room most of the time," I answered, as I sat down on the edge of the bed testing the softness. "How many times a year do you suppose they have newlywed couples anyway?"

"You're probably right," he answered, taking up my merriment. "I'll take the one closest to the door." Then smiling he set down the bags and took me in his arms and kissed me. "That way I'll have a head start should I want to escape," he concluded.

I put my hands on his chest and teasingly pushed myself free from his hold. "Actually, I want to be able to get there first to bar your way, so you can't escape," he said, trying to redeem himself.

We were both exhausted. It had been a long day, full of eager excitement, bustling activities, and then the long drive. The uninterrupted time had been nice. We had rehearsed all the day's events, but it had left us even more tired and anxious for rest.

Chuck picked up the suitcases and set them on the luggage racks. He opened his up, grabbing some clean skivvies, and headed for the bathroom. "Care to join me for a shower?" he asked, with a sound of hope in his voice. "I'll wash your back," he continued to bribe.

"No, thank you," I replied, "we'd never make it to the bed." I opened my own case and took out a beautiful white lacy negligee my sister Dorothy had given me several months before the wedding.

I shook out the negligee and laid it on the bed and began to get undressed. I heard Chuck's invitation again, over the sound of the water as he called out, "Sure you won't join me?" And then he started whistling the "Wedding March."

I chuckled at his good humor as I slid into the sexy feminine gown. I was folding my clothes and putting them away as Chuck emerged from the bathroom, dressed in his white Marine skivvies with his name and serial number stamped on both his shorts and t-shirt. He gave a soft wolf whistle and grabbed me a second time, kissing me passionately.

"Dressed like a bridegroom, I see," I teased, pulling on his t-shirt.

"Turns you on, doesn't it?" He chuckled stepping back and turning around. Free from his hold, I grabbed my cosmetic case and scurried to the bathroom.

While I finished getting ready for bed, Chuck investigated the T.V. while putting away his own things and folding down the covers on one of the beds.

When I came out, he was sitting against the headboard, propped up on the pillows, watching the tube. Without glancing up, he threw me a "You'll have to wait until this is over." Then, glancing in my direction, he grinned and hopped from the bed, flipping off the T.V. He took my arm and escorted me back to the bed. "Mmmmmmmm, you smell good. You look as beautiful, M'Liss, as the bride I married today." He stepped back for a better view and then turned the light switch off. As my eyes adjusted, I heard him moving around in the dark. Then I saw his silhouette as he took off his clothes and climbed in beside me. He felt fresh and warm from his shower, and I cuddled into his arms.

"This is pretty to look at," he said, foundling my negligee between his fingers. "but mighty cumbersome when making love."

I sat up and slipped it off over my head and dropped it to the floor. Then I snuggled back under the covers into Chuck's arms.

Like most newlyweds, we were nervous, naive, and anxious to please and satisfy each other. Yet I had no idea that Chuck's expectation for that night was to have a perfect sexual experience. Knowing we were both inexperienced and uninstructed, I didn't share the same anticipation.

Our foreplay was too short, and Chuck was unable to hold back his climax. When he realized I hadn't come, he was instantly angry, feeling inadequate, having fallen short of his anticipated goal.

As I lay there under him, he raised up on his one arm and started slapping me about the face and shoulders with his free hand. I was dumbstruck, bewildered. I tried to pull away, but I was pinned. I screamed and he hit me again crying, "Why did you rush me?"

I laid there speechless. How had I rushed him? I felt confused, perplexed, chaotic.

"I wanted you to come first," he continued in a voice of defeat, still holding me under him.

"Chuck," I sobbed, "it's okay, I didn't need to come, I wanted you to be satisfied."

He hit me again and then rolled off, stung, provoked, pulling the covers off us as he went. "How do you think I feel, coming and not satisfying you?" he snapped. "Do you think I'm that selfish?" He believed he had failed, and that left him feeling incompetent, insufficent. Those feelings frightened him and his reaction was to lash out in self-defense.

Free from his hold, I got out of bed. I caught up my negligee and stumbled to the bathroom, whimpering, "You can't expect to get it all right the first time, Chuck. I'm okay with not coming."

I locked the door behind me, and leaned against it sobbing into the negligee I held in my hands. I could hear Chuck getting out of bed, searching for the light. Then he came to the door and pulled hard on it, ordering me to come out.

I was still standing against the door when I felt it vibrate behind me. I straightened up and tried to clear my thoughts.

What had just happened was still a shock to me. Never in our fourteen months of dating had Chuck hit me. This was the last thing I had expected to happen. I was unprepared. What was I to do? I was two hundred and fifty miles from what had been home, my apartment. I had no friends here whom I could call for help. I didn't know where I was in relation to anything else. What could I do? If I were to leave, where would I go? Could I get my clothes and escape?

The door shook again and this time, Chuck's voice was calmer and more pleading. "Please let me in M'Liss. I don't know what got into me. Please open the door."

I saw no other alternative but to trust him. Yet, I still stood there unable to move, trying to interpret what had just happened, and what I could do about it.

Again he pleaded, "I'm sorry, M'Liss, I just had such high hopes and expectations for this moment. I felt like I blew it when I failed to satisfy you. Please forgive me and come out."

I moved away from the door and started putting my negligee back on. I switched on the light and grabbing a wash rag, I rinsed off my face. As I looked up from the sink to the mirror, I saw my eyes swollen from crying, my face red from Chuck's slaps. I replaced the rag, and opened the door to find Chuck still standing there waiting for me with an anxious, pathetic, look on his face. He held his arms open to me, and I rushed into them. "Please, forgive me," he implored again. "I didn't mean to do that M'Liss. I feel so ashamed, first for not satisfying you, and then for having hit you. Did I hurt you?" he asked, with tenderness in his voice. He stepped back to look at my face. Then, shaking his head in self-condemning disdain, he pulled me back into his arms.

"Why did you have to hit me, Chuck?" I knew there was no explanation to be heard. My dreams had been shattered, my hopes and expectations crushed.

CHAPTER 5

This behavior became a pattern that occurred and reoccurred over the next twenty years. At first, I thought it was a fluke, that it would never happen again. But I was mistaken. It was to become the norm, Chuck's way of handling disagreements, stress, failure, disappointments, and criticism.

When I thought of leaving, I was faced with the question, "Where can I go?" I was in unfamiliar territory. I certainly would never consider going back home to my sister's. The thought of facing my family and telling them Chuck had beaten me up on our honeymoon was too humiliating for me to face. I could hear the jeers, "I told you so, see, he was no good." I couldn't handle that. My apartment was gone. What could I do? I loved Chuck, and unlike my sister, he at least acknowledged the wrong of what he had done and said he was sorry. I would rather face the future with him hoping it would never happen again, as he said, than to go back to where I had been.

At first it really seemed like things were going to improve. After we arrived at his duty station and settled in, our life together was pleasant and enjoyable. We shared the same interests and did everything together. We loved movies, and could go often and cheaply there on base. We fished together, took rides in the country on his motor scooter, played cards with friends, and just sat together and watched T.V. I helped him with his studies and worked at a bank to subsidize our income. Things went smoothly until the day he decided to lend his motor scooter to a friend.

He didn't know the fellow very well, and the scooter was not always reliable. In the middle of nowhere, for no apparent reason, it would die. To get it started again, Chuck would have to take the carburetor apart, clean it, and put it back together before it would go. Chuck explained this problem to his friend and lent him the scooter. When I came home from work and heard what he'd done, I was upset and scared. It wasn't insured and we were liable if anything should happen. If the scooter were to break down, I was afraid he wouldn't be able to fix it properly. In anger, I expressed my fears and disapproval to Chuck. He in turn, remembering what would happen to him as a child when he made a mistake, or did something wrong, lashed out at me. He was scared. As far as he knew, what his parents did to him, I would do. I was mad, and he was afraid. So, he started hitting me. I criticized him for doing that, telling him he was taking his anger with himself out on me. This made him desperate. He took his webbed service belt and started whipping me with it. He hit me again and again. When I would try to get away, he would knock me down and lash me some more. I had welts all over my body, on my legs and arms, and especially across my back, seat, and thighs. They were red and purple where the blood vessels had broken. He kept beating me until he was exhausted and collapsed into a chair. I lay on the floor crying, too weak to get up and leave. There was no need to leave, he was done. I knew he wouldn't do anything more.

The man who had borrowed the scooter was late coming back. When he arrived, he told Chuck the scooter had broken down and that he had had to take the carburetor apart. When his friend was gone, Chuck apologized for the way he had treated me. He tenderly rubbed lotion on my bruises to help ease their soreness. He acknowledged how foolish he had been to loan the scooter out in the first place. It was this remorseful, repentant attitude that kept my faith in him alive. He was so rational after an explosion. He could see and acknowledge his errors, even if he wasn't able to correct them at the time. I knew the desire was there even if the will and motivation were not.

The next day, the scooter wouldn't go for Chuck. After taking the carburetor apart himself, he found that his friend had put it back together wrong and had chipped it. It never ran the same after that.

When Chuck completed his schooling, he was assigned a new duty station in Yuma, Arizona. We packed up our things and headed West, taking our time. We camped along the way, enjoying the sights as we went. We settled into a nice apartment and I again went to work at a bank. Chuck's work arrangement on base was such that he would be on duty for twenty four hours and off for forty-eight. He worked on the flight line refueling and parking aircraft. Most of the time, there were no flights coming in at night, so he was able to get a normal night's rest. Consequently, he would come home in the morning, rested and ready to go for the day. While I was working, he would spend the time fishing, riding his motor scooter, visiting friends, etc. When I got home each evening, I was faced with the responsibility for supper, cleaning, washing, etc. Before long, I became tired and discouraged from the load. I went to Chuck and asked him for help with some of the housework. He argued with me saying he needed the time off to rest. He thought he did his share by keeping up with the car maintenance and taking out the trash each day. I began to argue back, criticizing him for watching too much television when he could be helping with the dishes. I found fault with his sleeping during the day and then not making the bed when he got up. I angrily accused him of leaving his clothes laying around and expecting me to pick them up. As I pressed in on him more and more, he became frightened, feeling emasculated. He turned on me in defiance, like a cornered animal. In an uncontrolled rage, he attacked me, lashing out with blows of fury, first at my ribs and then my head. With his fists, he struck me in the chest. The wind was knocked out of my lungs in a gush. I doubled over, gasping for air. As I leaned toward him, he hit me across the face with one hand, and up the side of the head with the other. My glasses went sailing across the room, and at the same time a stream of blood started flowing from my ear.

At the sight of the blood, Chuck stopped, instantly snapping back to reality. He had gone too far. In defensive alarm, he started accusing me of being unreasonable and unrelenting; stating that I had pushed him beyond his limit. I accepted the blame, believing that I had indeed been forceful in my case against him. He went to the bathroom and got a rag. As he gently washed my face and ear, he apologized for his abuse and even offered to help out once in awhile with the dishes, or by making the bed.

My ear continued bleeding off and on the rest of the day and through the night. The next day, I went to the doctor to have it examined. When he asked me what had happened, I was too ashamed to admit I had nagged my husband and he had beaten me, so I lied. I invented a story about jabbing a "Q" tip in too far. Chuck's shifting the blame onto me had been effective. My own conscience condemned me. I believed it was my own fault. Thus, I took on the responsibility for Chuck's behavior. My victimization was complete.

Still, we pressed on in hope. Yet it became our way of life. How do I explain it? How do I remember it? Even as it happened, I could remove myself, by placing my mind across the room so it felt like I was looking on, rather than experiencing the blows. It's painful to recall.

Things would go along smoothly for a period of time with just small eruptions here and there. The tension would build and to divert it, I would be as compliant and nurturing as I could. I would try to anticipate all of Chuck's needs and be there to meet them. If he thought I failed, or something went wrong, if we disagreed, or I complained, he would then explode with physical abuse. During this explosion period, he would be irrational, out of control, and there was nothing I could say or do to calm him. His anger would have to run its course. Then, he would be remorseful and apologetic, promising it wouldn't happen again.

As the years flew by, I became more and more convinced that I was responsible for being beaten. It was my own fault. This was reinforced by our friends as well as our fellow church members. On several occasions when I shared Chuck's abuse with friends, I was met with criticism. "If you didn't talk back to him, he wouldn't do that." I was met with judgement. "If you were a better wife, he wouldn't have anything to be angry about." I was met with discrimination. "If you were submissive, he wouldn't have to hit you to keep you in line." Feeling overwhelmed by these accusations, I learned to keep silent. At church, I was met with indifference. "That's too bad." Or, "You know M'Liss," I would be warned, "it's a sin to divorce for any reason but adultery." Or, "You need to try harder to be a better wife." Only once in twenty years was anything said directly to Chuck. On that occasion I had been obviously abused and the minister took him aside and told Chuck he thought what he was doing was wrong and that he needed to get some help. Chuck disregarded this counsel, thinking that he was getting two different messages. On the one hand he was hearing that his wife should be submissive, and on the other hand, that his method was wrong. He didn't know any other way to reconcile the two and seeing no alternatives, he chose to ignore the advice. I grew hopeless and discouraged. I saw no way to stop him. The indifference of the first policeman I encountered when I finally charged Chuck was typical of the attitude I had been confronted with for twenty years.

Periodically, Chuck would get really depressed and comment that we weren't going to make it, meaning our marriage wasn't going to last. He would criticize me for not being a good wife, accuse me of nagging him too much, or of being too critical of him. Then that old scary feeling of being alone would grip me and I would try even harder to do better. The only solution seemed to be divorce. But for me, divorce meant abandonment and failure. It meant I was deficient as a person. *I'm unlovable.* It signified I was incompetent as a wife. *I'm not good enough.* And it suggested my missing the mark as a Christian. "I'm a sinner." Divorce seemed out of the question.

As long as no one was willing to confront Chuck and I couldn't accept divorce, he had free reign. There was no hope, no way out. I had to make it or die at Chuck's hand trying. Besides, I loved Chuck deeply, and he loved me. Apart from the violence, we had a good relationship. We still did everything together and shared the same interests. Our sex life improved, and we were more than comfortable with each other.

We had been in Arizona for two years when Chuck was ordered overseas. Since I had no home to go back to, we decided it would be best for me to remain there until his return. I became pregnant just before he left, and while he was gone our first child was born. Rebecca was four months old when Chuck came home. Things went smoothly when he first got back, but slowly, the old patterns of behavior began to surface again. Something would go wrong, I would be blamed and then he would explode. I accepted it as readily as I had before, believing I had it coming, that I needed to try harder, to do better.

A year after his return from overseas, he was discharged. Again we packed our belongings. We took our time and traveled up the West Coast, across Canada, and then down into Minnesota where we planned to make our home. We rented a little house and shortly after we settled in, our second daughter, Rachel, was born. Four years after her came our son, Elgin. Chuck got a good job, and we bought a house. We found a church to our liking and to those looking in our life seemed to be healthy and normal. We looked like a lovely happy family. For the most part that was true. I loved Chuck, and when he wasn't abusive, I was happy. Life was all that I had ever hoped for, or dreamed of, and so much better than where I had come from. Apart from the abuse, he was a good man. Though I would have liked for Chuck to be more involved with the children, he was supportive of me in the activities I engaged in with them. The scene was only disrupted if something went wrong, if someone made a mistake, or if something was lost or broken. Then all hell could break loose.

Chuck was never abusive to our girls. When our son was about six years old, Chuck began using him as a scapegoat. He treated Elgin with the same attitude his dad had shown towards him. I was afraid that Chuck would cause Elgin to hate him as he did his father, and I began to intervene. This only caused more stress and resentment. As our children grew, they too added to the tension that brought on some of the abuse. If they did something wrong, it was my fault. My survival depended on keeping them in line while making few mistakes myself. Often, Chuck never knew if they had broken a window, lost some tool, or failed a class. It was safer for me to keep it to myself and handle it without consulting him.

Subconsciously I lived in constant awareness of his disposition. It was my survival. Over the twenty years of our marriage, through various battles, I experienced black eyes, broken glasses, beatings, bruises, twisted arms, pulled hair, sexual abuse, attempted stranglings (with a belt on one occasion), many times with his hands around my throat.

If I sensed he was in a bad mood, I walked on egg shells, knowing that anything could upset that delicate balance. As the children got older, I no longer had time for watching T.V. My time was used in keeping things out of his way, the kids in line, and having whatever it was he wanted ready for whenever he wanted it. Just the slamming of a door when he came in put me on guard. The dropping of a pan could cause me to freeze momentarily, wondering if that would be the straw to break the camel's back. All my senses were alert and attuned to Chuck. His needs were my responsibility and I had better pay attention to be prepared to meet them when he wanted.

After ten years of marriage, Chuck did consent to seeing a psychiatrist. I put all my hopes into this, thinking it was the solution I had been hoping for. Our first visit quickly revealed that this was going to be a long slow process. It would take the doctor a lot of time to learn our backgrounds. We didn't talk much about the violence. That was too scary for me and too embarrassing for Chuck. So after we left that first day, I went home and wrote a lengthy letter sketching our history, starting with our courtship, and on through to the present, explaining our relationship and describing some of the violence.

With my letter to go on, the doctor began our treatment. We saw him together for about four visits. Then he started to see Chuck alone. Chuck went for about six years, but the subject of abuse was never directly addressed. Since there was little known about the cycle of violence at that time, his treatment was of little help. The abuse never stopped.

Eventually, Chuck resolved that he would not go back. When I questioned him about it, he said he felt embarrassed having to tell the doctor he had hurt me again. Besides, he thought the doctor had helped him all he could.

So the violence continued. Occasionally, when I recognized Chuck getting more and more uptight, and I sensed he was about to explode, I would subconsciously provoke him to get it over with, and bring the tension level down to a more tolerable balance.

Finally one night Chuck got really upset with me for something and started hitting. I managed to get out of the house slamming the door behind me, thus obstructing his way and giving myself some distance. I ran to the garage, locked the door and started the car as quickly as I could. As I backed out of the garage, Chuck came around the side of the building and started to climb our five foot chain link fence to catch me. I was able to pull away just as he got over. I drove for several miles and then stopped at a phone booth. I called the psychiatrist at his home. When I told him Chuck was really out of control and I was scared, he suggested I call him at his office the next morning and come in to see him. I was appalled. God help me, I thought, what was I to do right now? Yet I accepted his indifference as naturally as I had everyone else's for the past sixteen years. I hung up the phone and drove around some more. Eventually, I found myself in front of the local police station. I contemplated going in, but, when I thought of what I would say, what evidence I had, I believed there was nothing they could do. So I spent the night in a parking lot shivering with the cold. In the morning when I was sure Chuck had left for work, I went back home.

As soon as the children were off to school, I called the doctor's office and made an appointment to see him that afternoon. When I arrived and was seated comfortably, he inquired how things were going. When I explained that things were better, but there were still times of violence, he suggested I have Chuck come back to see him. I told him Chuck refused. He then acquainted me with a new law in Minnesota that would allow the police to arrest a man for abuse, even if they didn't witness the crime. He assured me that this new ruling gave teeth to the law and police were taking domestic assault more seriously than in the past. He then advised me to call the police and charge Chuck the next time he was abusive. I promised him that I would. He next wrote Chuck a note telling him that he had instructed me to do this. I went home, note in hand determined that should Chuck hit me again, I would in fact go to the police.

I showed Chuck the note, and announced my intentions. I even hung it on his dresser where it remained for many months. I also disclosed this to two of our couple friends in Chuck's presence. I vowed to them that if Chuck were abusive to me again, I would have him charged. They all expressed support and assured Chuck that they would encourage me to report him. My intention, if I had to resort to such a drastic measure, was to get Chuck to seek counseling again.

With that, Chuck "behaved." The rampages stopped. It lasted for a year, until we were in Canada on vacation. As we pulled into the campground, he became upset. It wasn't even clear to me what it was about, but he started hitting me in the car. What could I do? We were out of the country. I let it go.

There was peace again for another year. Then when we were on vacation in Missouri, it happened again.

Something went "wrong," and I was punished. What could I do? This time we were out of the state.

When we returned home, Chuck started getting more and more aggressive. No real hitting, just a little pushy, a shove here, a jostle there. Nothing specific you could classify as abuse. He was being careful not to go too far. It felt like he was testing the limits, leaning on the walls.

Then came the incident in the car when we were going to see our friend in the hospital. He had done it. He had crossed the line. Finally there was evidence. Finally I could prosecute if I had the courage and the support to do it.

CHAPTER 6

My decision to charge Chuck with abuse was one that reflected my growing perception that I had some control over my life. The trip to the police station was the culmination of nearly thirty years of helplessness and struggle, and I was both hesitant in believing in my chances of success and confident that I was going to follow through. I was determined to try to change the direction of our lives.

The three weeks following that initial visit were traumatic. I was required to provide proof of the abuse in the form of photographs and medical records. The photographs made it necessary for me to enlist the aid of one of my daughters. So, my first announcement of what I was doing was to Rachel. She helped by taking the picture of my bruised arm for the police and her encouraging support helped me through the long waiting period. The initial investigation was at last completed, and the city agreed to take my case. It meant that Chuck would be indicted and would have to face a hearing, and possibly stand trial.

Telling Chuck what I had done and what he would have to face would be the hardest part of the whole situation. I wanted so badly for him to admit his guilt, acknowledge his need for help, and say he wanted to change, that he cared enough about our family to make an effort. But Chuck was a defensive, violent person, and I knew there was a strong possibility of a major scene when he found out. And even though I thought he would eventually calm down, I was afraid of the initial blow-up. For my own safety and that of the children, I asked Ron and Nancy, our dearest friends, and one of the two couples I had previously told I would charge Chuck should he ever be abusive again, to come and be with me when I broke the news. I also hoped they could help Chuck to see my action in a positive light, and to offer him their assistance in getting through what was going to be a rough time for all of us.

Ron arrived a little after eight on the evening we had selected for telling Chuck. He explained that Nancy was detained at work and would be over in a little while. Chuck was unsuspecting. I left him and Ron visiting in the living room and busied myself with other things until the doorbell rang.

I answered the door in relief and ushered Nancy into the living room to a seat on the couch next to Ron. Chuck stood up to greet her, and we all chatted a few moments, the kind of warm, casual interaction we had shared together for several years. It was tempting for me to just relax and continue the evening as we had so often done before. Why make waves? And yet, the decision had already been made. I had to follow through. Nevertheless, I probably would have stalled a little longer if Nancy hadn't taken the situation into hand.

She had been leaning comfortably back on the couch. Now, in a fairly decisive movement, she sat up, and turned toward Chuck.

"Ron and I are here for a specific reason, Chuck," she said quietly. "I don't feel comfortable making small talk with what's ahead of us tonight." She paused, and Chuck looked at her, his eyebrows lifted, questioning.

Nancy continued, looking at me this time. "I'd like to see you, M'Liss, get to the point of our visit."

This was it. I was thrown into the ring. I had no choice but to take the challenge. I tried to calm myself by taking a couple of deep breaths. Then I turned and spoke directly to Chuck. "I've asked Ron and Nancy over tonight Chuck, because I have some awkward news. I think we're going to need their reinforcement."

Chuck edged forward on his chair, an unsuspecting, puzzled look on his face. I now had his complete attention. I went on before he could speak. "After you beat me up last month, I went to the police and filed a charge against you for assault."

Chuck stared, tilting his head slightly, as if trying to hear me better, trying to comprehend what I had just said.

"After looking into the matter, the city has agreed to prosecute, Chuck."

"You've what?" he exclaimed, half rising from his chair.

I forged ahead. "You're going to have to appear in court. They'll tell you when. Please understand, Chuck," I begged, "I don't want to hurt you. I'm just using the court to force you into getting some help. I want the abuse to stop."

He continued to glare at me for a moment, a penetrating stare, his eyes growing cold and hard. When he finally spoke, his words were sharp, loud, and icy.

"How could you be so stupid? You've sealed your own fate, M'Liss. What makes you think I would stick around for that? I'm leaving. I'm catching the first bus out of here and I'm never coming back." He paused, breathing heavily for a few seconds.

We all sat, silent, waiting.

When he spoke again, his voice sounded bullying. "You can have the kids, the house, the car, the whole bit. I'm through with you, M'Liss. You unappreciative bitch. Let's see how you do on your own." His face became dark red as his emotions intensified and redoubled again. The veins on his neck pushed to the surface. He appeared completely out of control.

Then, with a sudden lunge, he was on his feet. Like a shot, he was out the living room door, through the kitchen, and tearing down the basement stairs to Rebecca's room. She was doing her homework, oblivious to the uproar. Although I had forewarned her and Rachel of what I was going to do, she started as he burst through her door, suddenly realizing what must be happening.

"Rebecca," Chuck erupted, "I'm leaving. Your mother is ungrateful. She doesn't appreciate anything I've done for her." He paused for a moment, catching his breath, his chest heaving. "Do you know what she's done? She's charged me with abuse! She thinks she's so smart. Let's see how well she can do on her own!" With that, he turned and vaulted back up the stairs, taking them two at a time. He was impetuous, completely irrational.

Rebecca screamed and came tearing up the stairs after him. "No, Daddy," she begged. "I love you, Daddy, please don't go, please don't go."

Chuck froze in his tracks. She threw her arms around him as if to restrain him from leaving. Responding to her affection, he murmured, "I know, Rebecca, I know you love me." He patted her back and smoothed her long hair. "But your mother thinks she's got it all worked out—and I'm not staying around for it to happen."

The gentle side of Chuck had always been there for Rebecca, and now she spoke to him out of her love. "Please, Daddy. When I was little, if I was naughty, you spanked me, and I learned to be good," she reasoned, hugging him tightly to her. "Maybe you need to learn not to hit. I don't want you to leave us, Daddy," she continued as she sobbed against his shoulder. Chuck pushed her gently away, but his voice was harsh and determined. "There's no changing my mind." He turned and made his way down the hall to Rachel's bedroom door. Without knocking, he opened it and thundered in at her, "I'm leaving, Rachel. I'm leaving and I'm never coming back." Rachel, half asleep, looked up at him in confusion as he withdrew from the doorway and proceeded back to the living room.

In a flash, she was out of bed. She flew through the doorway and came down the hall after him. "You have it coming, Dad," she shouted, her voice trembling with anger. "You can't just go around beating up people whenever you feel like it and not expect someone to eventually do something about it." She looked at Rebecca, still crying across the room. "Dad, do you want us to run away every time we get in trouble for doing something wrong? You can't run away, Dad."

Chuck stared at her in disbelief. Here was the contrast in his daughters, the one mothering him, the other insisting he take responsibility for his actions. Each one represented a dimension of my own feelings and behavior toward Chuck.

"Come on, Dad," Rachel reasoned, her voice more pleading by now. "What do you expect Mother to do, just let you hit her anytime you feel like it? Can't you see, Dad, she has to do this?"

By the time Rachel finished, Rebecca had stopped crying and Chuck was standing in the doorway to the living room from the hall. Ron, Nancy, and I had remained seated in suspended animation while all this had been going on. Now Ron, rising from the couch turned to Chuck. "Come on Chuck, let's you and I go out for a walk and talk for awhile."

Chuck shook his head, not looking at any of us. "I don't want to talk Ron. There's no changing my mind. Let her just find out how she does without me."

"Come on Chuck," Ron continued, ignoring Chuck's

statement, "let's go have something to eat, or for a drive. Just at least let us talk about it for a moment."

Without answering Ron, Chuck whirled around and darted into the kitchen. He rushed over to the desk, and took out all of our blank checks. Then, grabbing my billfold from my purse, he brought them into the living room and stopped in front of me. I sat paralyzed. He began ripping up the checks, throwing them at me as he worked. Then he took the credit cards from my billfold, and bent them in half, and threw them on the floor at my feet. "There," he spat out, "see how you get along now. But I'm not footing the bill. Make your own way since you think you're so smart and high and mighty. You do it." Then, he turned to Ron, "I'll go out with you Ron, but you won't change my mind."

Ron had been standing since Chuck first came back to the living room. Now he reached for his coat on the back of the couch, as Chuck went to the closet to get his. Chuck stalked out and Ron followed, closing the door behind them.

I sat in my chair, stunned by his reaction. I never dreamed he would take it this hard. His threat of leaving hadn't even crossed my mind. I sat there in a state of disbelief and shock. I felt panicked and immobilized. Around my feet lay all the torn checks. In the doorway stood the girls, tears still on Rebecca's cheeks, Rachel shaking in her nightgown.

Nancy's voice broke the stillness, "You were great, all of you, just great." Her voice was full of pride and excitement. "Ron can handle Chuck, don't worry," she continued reassuringly, as she stood up and crossed the room to the girls. She put her arms around both of them, drawing them close to her.

I had not told Elgin anything about what I was doing and I remembered him now. I was concerned that he would be frightened by all he had heard. I got up and went down to the basement, where his room was. He was laying quietly in bed, but he was wide awake. "Elgin, did you hear what went on upstairs?" I asked anxiously.

Elgin looked at me bewildered. "I heard Daddy yelling that he was going to leave." He choked back a sob. "Is he really going to leave? What's the matter, Mother?"

I sat down on the edge of his bed and tried to explain what I had done, why I hadn't told him, and why Daddy was reacting as he was. "Elgin, sweetheart," I asked tentatively, "would you like to come upstairs for a while? We can all be together that way?" He nodded, scrambling from his bed. I took his hand and led him up to the living room.

Nancy was sitting on the couch with the girls next to her. She was rubbing their backs and cuddling them in a reassuring manner. Elgin, coveting her affection too, quickly joined them. We all sat and talked together, trying to sooth and bolster each other, the kids crying and expressing their fears and anger. After about an hour, the children all went back to their beds, still feeling somewhat apprehensive, but a little better. I hoped they would be able to sleep.

Nancy and I continued talking, speculating about what was happening with the men, and what would happen when they came back.

Shortly after one o'clock, the door opened. I wasn't sure Chuck would return at all, but now they were here, taking their places in the living room where they had been before. So much had transpired since we had all first started talking, it was incomprehensible. Chuck was still cold and harsh, but he seemed to have calmed down some.

He leaned back in his chair, and closed his eyes for a moment. When he spoke, his voice sounded controlled and rational. "Okay, M'Liss, tell me what's going to happen."

Encouraged, I began to explain. "The city will send you a letter in the mail, Chuck. It will formally announce the charge and tell you when you're to appear for a hearing."

Chuck slammed his fist against the arm of the chair, but said nothing.

Ron spoke. "Chuck, if you want, Nancy and I will come to the hearing with you." He looked at Nancy for corroboration. She nodded. Ron continued, "You have our support all the way Chuck, if you want it."

Chuck nodded, but again didn't speak for several seconds. Then he looked at me. "What else, M'Liss?"

At least he was sane enough to ask questions. "Well, Chuck, it's my understanding that if you plead guilty, you'll be assigned a court investigator." I tried to sound confident. "You'll meet with the investigator for an interview. He'll then make a recommendation to the judge, based on the interview. You'll be given a second court date for sentencing."

Chuck was calm, but he wasn't buying it. "You think it's that simple, M'Liss. Do you realize this could cost me my job?" His fist began to rhythmically pound the arm of the chair. "Whatever were you dreaming of to think the courts are going to let me off that easy? How naive can you be?"

I could see he was starting to get worked up again, so I quickly responded, "I'm sure you won't lose your job or be put in jail, Chuck. All I've asked is that you be required to get some counseling. That's it, Chuck."

For the first time since he had returned with Ron, he raised his voice, his face turning red again as he barked, "You're a fool if you think that's what will happen!"

"Chuck," Ron began, "let's just wait and see. Take it one step at a time, okay? Nancy and I will be there. All the court is interested in is to see that you get help. They don't want you to lose your job. That would defeat their purpose too. They're just interested in seeing that this kind of behavior doesn't continue, that's all." He leaned forward and gripped Chuck's knee for a moment in a gesture of sympathy and encouragement. "I really think M'Liss is right. They don't want you in jail. They just want you to change your conduct."

Chuck relaxed a little, responding to Ron's sincerity. "I hope you're right, Ron. I'm depending on it."

It was an exhausting night for all of us. I felt apprehensive when Ron and Nancy stood up to leave. I was afraid Chuck's temper might flare again once we were alone. When I expressed my misgivings, he insisted he was resolved. It seemed he had shut down for the night, at least. So for the time being, things were left at simmer on the back burner.

CHAPTER 7

A series of bizarre conversations between Chuck and me followed over the next several days as Chuck tried to adjust to what was happening. One day shortly after "the encounter," Chuck called and asked me to pick him up after work. He said he wanted to take me out to dinner. I was suspicious. I felt uncomfortable.

I picked him up promptly and we headed for a quiet Oriental restaurant across town. After we were comfortably seated at a small table, Chuck announced that he had decided to move out and possibly get a divorce. I felt a shot go through me like an arrow. I gasped for air feeling the impact of his words. But I quickly realized I was being manipulated. "Chuck," I replied, "I don't think it's necessary for you to do that, but if that's what you think you want to do, I won't try to stop you."

I couldn't believe my answer. How could I say that? I had always been terrified at the thought whenever Chuck threatened to leave. Yet, it was the exact position I needed to take. It was the very reply Chuck did not anticipate or want. If I didn't respond as in the past, full of fear, begging him not to leave, what would he do next?

Confronted with what seemed to be indifference from me, Chuck was forced to discuss the pros and cons of his moving out. He supposed he would get a one-room apartment and bury himself in T.V. He didn't think he would take up drinking or women, but he did intend to do whatever he wanted for a change, without me to nag and bitch at him.

Next, we analyzed my living alone and what I would do. I observed that I would want to remarry. This thought seemed to distress him. He expressed that his greatest apprehension was that I would marry a loser, someone worse than himself. We debated back and forth about the likelihood of that, since I would be saddled with three children, two of them adolescents. At ten, we left the restaurant and went to a bar until midnight. It was the first time we had ever gone to a bar to drink, and the atmosphere felt as strange as our conversation. When the bar closed, we sat in the car in a park, making love. This was something I had asked Chuck to do for years. Why did it take a charge of assault, the threat of divorce, and the fear of losing one another to bring us to do what we should have been doing all along? By one in the morning, we had resolved to remain together for the time being.

On another day, we sat together in the car waiting for Elgin to finish his orchestra practice. Chuck started in, as usual: What was I ever thinking of to have charged him in the first place? Did I really know what I was doing? Should he or should he not move out? Finally, I had had enough. I turned to him in my seat and declared in an impatient voice, "Chuck, all I hear you talking about is yourself, and how this is hurting you and threatening your job. I'm being treated like it's my fault you were cited, like I'm responsible for what you're going through. But you're forgetting or ignoring and denying that it was your own actions that brought this on."

I shook with indignation. "Have you thought at all about what it has been like for me and how I feel right now? All I've heard is you crying, blaming, and threatening. I haven't seen you take a look at yourself once yet." I finished in tears and we sat in silence.

After some minutes, Chuck reached over and took

my hand and said, "You're right M'Liss. I can't see the purpose of this at all. I feel helpless and vulnerable, it's all so out of my control. I only hope you know what you are doing."

I couldn't believe his response. He was rational, reasonable, even compassionate. I could love him forever when he was like that. Why did it have to take the extreme measure of discipline for him to be reasonable.

Elgin came out from his practice, and we drove home.

I thought we had finally made some progress. But I had expected too much too soon. The very next day we were back where we started. This time Chuck called from work on his lunch break. He started in again with the threat of moving out and getting a divorce. He had been talking with some of his fellow employees. They were telling him that he would probably have to spend some time in jail. This notion had renewed that old fear, casting doubt on all I had been telling him. Also, they were beginning to put pressure on him to get a lawyer, suggesting that the lawyer could arrange it so that he might be able to work in the day at his job and then go back to jail for the night. He hung up the phone sounding insecure, martyred by the exorbitant power the courts held over his future.

I spent the afternoon grooming dogs and meditating over the conversation we had had when Elgin was at orchestra practice, versus the one we had just concluded. The more I thought about it, the more disconcerted I felt. "He hasn't gotten the message yet," I mused to myself. Drumming my fingers with impatience, I dialed him back at work. "Parts room, please." I asked, my voice restrained.

"Parts room, Switzer speaking." came the reply.

"Chuck," I said still in control, "I hear you are worried and scared about losing your job. But I'm calling to tell you that you're concerned about the wrong thing. I'm a damn good wife, and you're about to lose me. You had better get your act together and your head screwed on right and decide what is more important to you, because I'm not hanging around much longer."

I didn't wait for a reply, I just hung up the phone. When he came home from work, I persisted, driving the point home. I said that before I would let him divorce me and leave me with the children, I would divorce him and he could raise the kids. I acquainted him with the fact that it would be far easier for him to remarry with three kids on his tail than for me. And, I would remarry. I had his undivided attention. "You always said," I continued, gathering steam, "when the kids were bigger, you'd spend more time with them, that the diaper and nursing scenes were my jobs. Well, they're bigger and now you can have your chance. I've spent a lot of time with them. I've built my relationships and I can afford to leave. They know who I am and how I feel about them. I don't need to impress that on them anymore. If there is to be a divorce, I'll be the one to get it."

This was to be one of our turning points. The stark reality that someone was going to have to change was before us both. There was another option besides his going into therapy: divorce. Was I ready for that? Jesus once said, "Once you set your hand to the plow, you should not look back." I hadn't realized when I first initiated the charge that this might end up being one of my options. I naively believed he would plead guilty, go in for some kind of therapy, the abuse would end, and we'd live happily ever after. But in the face of reality, Chuck wasn't seeing it the same way. For him, the issue was his job, while mine was change and an end to the violence.

Now that the charge was made, my turning back would mean being abused the rest of my life. It would be a life on his terms. My own self-respect, as well as any respect Chuck had left for me, would be lost. He would walk all over me if I relented now. It was either all or nothing, and I had made up my mind that afternoon while grooming the dogs in the basement that I had had enough. I did not want to be abused anymore. I was ready to pay the price of losing Chuck and my marriage if that was what it took to gain back some power and self-respect. I was ready to go all the way, but I was still going to hang in there and fight.

Chuck grasped the picture clearly. What could he say? Did he want divorce? He hadn't resolved that yet for himself. He gave no response. After this confrontation, life for us settled back into the old routine as if nothing had happened, as if no charge had been filed. We just kind of fell into limbo, deadened to what lay before us. We enjoyed a reprieve for a few days anyway.

At the same time this was going on with Chuck, I was engaged in another struggle with a woman from the church who had been a close friend for several years. She and her husband were the other couple I had told two years earlier that I would charge Chuck should he ever hurt me again. They had agreed to be supportive. I was counting on them now. The woman was older than I and very active in the church. She was a person I had been somewhat influenced by, both personally and in a couples group we both were involved with. I called her immediately after I charged Chuck and again when I learned the city had agreed to take the case. Shortly after, I invited her and her husband over for dinner. They expressed support indicating that they would stand by us. They told Chuck they believed his abusive behavior was wrong and needed to stop. Nevertheless, they cared about him and wanted to be there for him. It sounded good, but that was the extent of their advocacy. My friend never called after that to see what was happening, to see if we needed anything or to say she cared.

She and her husband were frequently out of town, busy with family and business responsibilities. I knew they had many commitments, and if she had told me she would not have time to give me the attention I needed, I could have let go and sought support elsewhere. But she didn't. When I would allude to her lack of interest, she would become defensive, reassuring me of her attention. Yet, that message started slowly coming through. When they were gone, we would occasionally get cute little cards, but when they returned, we didn't hear from them. At church, she would come up to us and ask how things were going, but it was casual—no different from others there who knew nothing of our struggles. Finally, I called her and tried to talk to her about what was happening with Chuck and me. But she seemed bored, or calloused, or indifferent. I didn't know which, only that she didn't want to talk about it. She would change the subject frequently—my impression was that she felt uncomfortable, but mostly uninterested. In general, I kept getting a double message; I received lip service, but no life service.

But the real disillusionment was yet to come. Rebecca was competing in a violin contest and had asked a girl-friend from church to accompany her on the piano. So, one night after church, Chuck and I went out with the girl's parents while she and Rebecca practiced. As we left the parking lot, I saw my friend observing us and thought it a little strange. But I quickly dismissed it as I became involved in our conversation. We had a pleasant evening and never brought up our problem.

The following week I learned my friend had called the girl's mother the day after we had been out. She then asked her if we had discussed our problem with them. When the girl's mother responded with a confused "No, I don't think so," my friend took it upon herself to "fill her in." I was stupefied and shocked. The rug had been pulled out from under me.

I related the predicament to Chuck and when he understood what had happened, he called my friend. He informed her that he had been made aware that she had talked about his abuse with the girl's mother. Then he asked her if that was true. She hesitated momentarily, then replied nervously that it wasn't. Chuck repeated quietly, "I'm going to ask you again, did you talk about us?" He could hear her gasp on the other end of the line. Sounding cornered and exposed, she responded that she had. Then attempting to vindicate herself, she explained that she was only trying to help. Chuck reminded her that she had been told what she knew in absolute confidence, and that he wanted her to understand unequivocally that she was not to discuss it again without his permission. Sounding shook up, she whispered that she was sorry, and again in an attempt to whitewash her actions, repeated that she was only trying to help.

I felt deceived, defrauded, battle-weary. While I was needing reassurance and support, I received indifference and betrayal. My circuits were already overloaded. This was too much. I needed space. Feeling fatigued, I backed away from her. Our friendship had been severely wounded.

CHAPTER 8

During the interval of time after the charge and before the hearing Chuck began looking at various options, not only separation and divorce, but treatment as
well. He discovered that there was a new program
called Domestic Abuse Project in Minneapolis that dealt
with our problem. He made further inquiries and
learned it was designed to help the entire family. When
he shared this with me I was elated. It was more than I
had even hoped for. We each made an appointment for
an intake interview. It was possible he could be signed
up before his trial, and that would stand in his favor.

He also learned that there was a Men's Self-Help
Group meeting once a week in Burnsville and that he
could go to that on a walk-in basis. It was part of the
Domestic Abuse Project Program. So, for a couple of
weeks before his trial, he attended this self-help group.
He felt favorably impressed and comfortable there. He
got to meet other men with the same problem and they
spent one evening a week confronting and encouraging
each other in their recovery.

In the meantime, the day for the hearing was quickly
approaching and with its advent, the tension was again
increasing. Chuck started renewing his threats of leaving and divorce and now he added a new one. Some of
the fellows he worked with were insisting he have some
kind of legal counsel. I was holding my breath, keeping

my eye fixed on the calendar, trying to hold things together until the hearing. If I could just stall him off until
then, I believed once the court proceedings began he
would calm down and see for himself that what I had
been saying was true. The court only wanted to see him
get help and change his behavior. Now with this new
threat of a lawyer, I felt overwhelmed, like holding back
a leaking dam. I'd no sooner shore up one place and another would break through. I believed without question
that a lawyer could get him off. If that happened, it
meant defeat for me. I equated it with the sergeant telling me I would have to wait until the next assault if the
city rejected my case. Chuck would see me and the system as a mockery. I might just as well crawl back in my
hole and pull the top in over me. I would lose and he
would be free to go on controlling me with threats and
fear even if he never hit me again.

A week before the hearing, he came home from work
all uptight and boisterous. "M'Liss, everyone at work
thinks I'm nuts to go to that hearing without a lawyer.
One of the fellows gave me a guy's name and I want to
go and see him. He says this guy is reasonable."

"Why do you need a lawyer, Chuck? I thought you
agreed to plead guilty. What good can he do you?" My
voice sounded weak as I reached for a chair to steady
myself. "And think what it will cost."

His rebuttal was quick and sharp. "The cost doesn't
matter since my job and reputation are at stake. If I lose
my job what difference would the cost be then? And
whether I plead guilty or not, I have nothing to lose by
consulting an attorney."

He was sounding hurried like he had to get it out before he lost it. Yet his stance seemed determined.

I feared resisting any longer, thinking he would get
out of control. Yet I believed I dare not weaken in my
position. "Just a week more," I told myself, "keep it together for just a week more." Then it would be over

and we would be on our way to getting help. Why couldn't he see that? Why must he keep fighting it like this?

"Chuck," I began softly yet with resolution, "just wait a little longer, just trust me. It will go as I said. Please wait."

He sulked away looking defeated. It was like he was going along on someone else's argument and it had run out.

The next day, he called me from work, sounding renewed and reinforced. He informed me he had made an appointment to see the lawyer after work, and he would be home late.

"What?" I gasped. I couldn't believe Chuck was going to go ahead and see him. I felt unable to stop him.

Adding to my panic, he continued, "I asked him if I should bring my wife along and he said absolutely not. I haven't anything to lose, M'Liss, by going and talking to him, so I'm going to give it a shot."

Everything felt out of my control. "Well, Chuck, do what you have to do, but I really wish you would leave him out of it. I'll see you when you get home."

The afternoon felt like an eternity. I didn't know what I was waiting for or what to expect. When he came home, I sensed he was upset and disconcerted. In a huff, he repeated what the lawyer had said. He had told Chuck he could get the charge changed from a felony to a misdemeanor. He even seemed to think he could get Chuck off all together. His fee was sixty dollars an hour and he estimated his time would be about ten hours.

I hit the roof. I felt undermined, destroyed. I was furious. In one quick sweep, he was going to undo everything for which I had worked so hard and risked so much. I was determined to fight back. "Chuck, six hundred dollars would pay for an awful lot of therapy. I didn't file charges against you to turn around and pay someone to get you off."

"Yes, but getting the charge changed to a misdemeanor would mean it wouldn't go on my record at work." Chuck retorted. "That's worth a lot to me."

"But six hundred dollars, Chuck, don't you feel a little like you're being ripped off?" I moved a step back from him as I spoke, knowing I was pushing hard and wanting distance for safety.

Looking embarrassed, Chuck relented. "Yes, I believe the price is too high and he's ripping me off. I haven't hired him yet. But at the same time, I feel like I'm cutting my own throat going into court without any representation." Then sounding helplessly defeated, he sunk down into a chair. "I just don't know what to do. I'm damned if I do, and I'm damned if I don't." Chuck went on to say he had told the lawyer that if he didn't use him for this trial, perhaps he would need him after, since he was also contemplating a divorce. He went on to say that the lawyer seemed confident that he would see Chuck again.

"I feel hatred for the man, whoever he is." I snarled with venom in my voice. "It's my impression that he is lining his pockets with my life and marriage. He isn't interested in seeing us get better, he's interested in revenue at someone else's expense. I wouldn't trust him for the time of day."

Our positions were clear, our battle lines drawn. The more we discussed the matter, the more exasperated Chuck became. Finally, he was so annoyed by my locked-in resistance that he called Ron and went over to talk to him. He was gone for several hours and when he returned, he was still outraged. He said that Ron had encouraged him to hire the attorney if that's what he thought he needed and had even offered to lend him the money.

I felt outnumbered. The opposition was getting stronger. It seemed everyone was against me. If this attempt to get Chuck in for help failed, what was there left for me to do? I couldn't give in now. The hearing was in two days. Could I stall him until then? "Well," I asked, trying to sound indifferent, "did you take him up on his offer?"

"No," he screamed with resentment, like he had no control of the outcome. You could almost see the struggle going on in him as he wrestled with his decision. "And I'm going against all my common sense. I didn't hire one because you say I don't need one. I'm a fool. Everyone says I'm a fool for not having one. I hate myself for not having one, but I don't want to spend the money."

One day to go. These past three months had been a contest all the way and it would carry us to the wire.

The next day Chuck came home from work and didn't mention the lawyer. He ate supper and got ready to go to his Men's Self-Help Group. I was relieved to have him gone. He would be distracted for a little while anyway. Just hang on until tomorrow, I kept telling myself over and over. It will all be ended then. The court system would begin its work and soon we could start our treatment.

I was reading in the living room when he came home. Without saying a word, he walked into our bedroom and went to bed. This was very unusual. I felt uneasy as I made my way around in the dark getting myself ready. He still hadn't spoken when I crawled in beside him.

My head no sooner hit the pillow when he asked, "Do you realize what you have done?" His voice was sharp and angry.

I was dumbfounded. "What are you talking about?" I inquired innocently.

With that question, all hell broke loose. He started yelling at me and at the same time began shoving me out of bed. "The men in my group have been after me all evening for not having a lawyer tomorrow. They think I'm indecisive and weak for not taking care of myself better than that. I let you talk me out of it and now here it is the last minute, and I am going to go to that court like a dumb asshole with no representation."

By this time I was on the floor. I scrambled to my feet and started for the door. He got there first. He locked it and pushing me on the chest, backed me around the room. "I hate you so much right now, I want to kill you. They should have never turned me loose tonight from group. They could see I was worked up." He had backed me up to the wall. "I'd like to just choke you to death right now. Why didn't you let me get a lawyer?"

I was terrified, how could I calm him down? In fear, I relented, "Call the lawyer in the morning and have him meet you there if you want."

"What makes you so agreeable now?" He raved as he grabbed my throat with his hands. "That's too much money you said. What makes you suddenly so generous?" As he spoke, he released his hold and pushed me away.

I persisted, trying to reason with him. "Chuck, we've been all through this. We can't do anything about it now. Everything will be okay, you'll see, it will be okay." My voice trailed off, he was leaving the room.

He continued muttering as he went, "I never do what I want. We always go by what you say. I let you walk all over me. I should have left the night you first told me and got it over with."

I stood by the bed stunned. After a moment, I gathered my wits about me and headed for the door and down the hall. Grabbing my purse, I made for the back door.

"Oh, no you don't." came his voice over my shoulder as he reached past me and locked the door. "Don't run away now, the party is just beginning." He shoved me back down the hall and toward the bedroom.

"Chuck, please calm down, it's going to be okay." I sounded like a broken record.

"Why didn't you investigate more before running to the police? There are other ways to get treatment without going to court. You could have done a lot more research before you had to stoop to this. This is all your fault. It wouldn't have happened if you had kept this to yourself."

I tried patronizing him. "You're right Chuck, I could have checked out other alternatives before going to the police."

I went back to the bed, feeling trapped. I got in and sat leaning against the headboard, exhausted, defeated, ready to give up, give in, whatever it took to bring these months of yo-yo existence to an end.

Chuck locked that door too. "Sure, now you want to leave. That's it, run away, leave me holding the bag."

"Chuck," I pleaded, waning under the strain, "in a few hours it will all begin and you'll see it will be just as I said. The court only wants to see you get help, Chuck." I had my eyes closed as I spoke and now I opened them and looked over at him sitting on the other side of the bed. I blinked in disbelief.

He was holding his grandfather's old gun with one hand and he was starting to load it with the other. I didn't move. "Chuck," I asked just above a whisper, "what are you doing?"

Without pausing he replied, "I'm going to kill myself." His voice was calm and even, resolved, like he had it all worked out.

"Chuck," I begged, "please don't do this." He had threatened suicide many times in our early years of marriage, but he had never gone this far.

"I can't face losing my job and I feel humiliated going to court unprepared like this. I should have done this in the beginning." His voice was desperate, full of turbulence and confusion.

There was a chance he was manipulating me again, but I sensed he was really ready to go through with it.

Without moving, I spoke to him soothingly. "I won't try to stop you, Chuck, it's your choice, but I beg you, please don't do this. It will all be all right Chuck. I know it will."

Shaking his head, he cried in broken tones, "What will I do? What will I do?" He laid the gun across his lap, his hands shaking.

"Please put it away Chuck. . . . " I pleaded, keeping my voice even and soft. Not daring to move a muscle, I sat paralyzed. He sat there too, quietly staring straight ahead. After a few moments, he started mumbling something. Then as though he had resigned himself, he reached for the case.

I realized I wasn't breathing because as he did so I gasped, trying to catch my breath. "Unload it please, Chuck." I whispered.

With hands still shaking, he opened the chamber and removed the bullet. "What's going to happen to me?" he sobbed desperately, "What's going to happen to me?"

I got up and went over and stood beside him, rubbing his shoulder with my hand as he put the gun in the case. "It will be okay, Chuck, you'll see."

Getting up, he set the gun in the closet corner. Then he came back to the bed and stood looking at me, shaking his head back and forth. "It's all over with, I should have left at the beginning. I hate myself for being so gutless. You've made a big mistake, M'Liss, thinking they're going to let me off as you say. You're a fool for trusting them, and I'm a bigger fool for trusting you."

He reached over and switched off the light. "Let's try to get some sleep before I'm fed to the lions."

CHAPTER 9

Chuck's hearing at the Adult Detention Center was scheduled for nine in the morning. When we arrived, we found Ron and Nancy already waiting for us. Together, we went into the attractive new building, glad to get out of the cold wind. After asking directions, we found our way down to the hearing room. We entered a low-ceilinged room filled with comfortable theater-type chairs arranged in rows, semi-circle fashion. The modern-looking chamber was decorated in gray and maroon. Attractive, natural finished tables lined the front of the room before the judge's bench.

We found a vacant row of seats and filed in. I could hardly breathe. We quietly took our seats and waited for the proceedings to begin.

A clerk appeared and announced the name of each person to be called to the bench. The indicted person responded with "here." Next he asked if anyone needed legal counsel. If so, they were to come forward and the court would appoint a lawyer. At this point, it was all Chuck could do to stay in his seat.

After these formalities were completed, the court was called to order. Everyone stood up and the judge entered. The hearings began. We sat wide-eyed, observing the parade of offenders being summoned to the bench as their specific crimes were read off. From all appearances, the judge seemed like a reasonable man, trying to administer justice to each offender who stood before him.

The clerk, reading off the charge as "a misdemeanor offense of domestic assault in the fourth degree," called Chuck to the bench. I couldn't believe my ears. I had understood all this time that his crime was a felony. As such, it would go on Chuck's work record and possibly jeopardize his job. He too had agonized over the previous weeks that if he didn't lose his job, a felony would certainly be held against him the next time he was considered for a promotion. I felt delivered. I was certain he too would be relieved and encouraged to hear this news, anyway.

Chuck rose, looking dignified in his light gray suit with his soft-colored tie. Going forward, he took his place respectfully before the judge.

Without looking up, the judge inquired, "How do you plead?"

Leaning forward slightly, Chuck responded clearly, "Guilty."

By this time, I was shaking from head to toe. Nancy reached over and grabbed my hand. My breath came in gasps.

Still not looking at Chuck, the judge replied, "I consign you to a probation officer for a pre-trial investigation. After stating your case to the investigator, you'll be scheduled a second hearing date, for sentencing."

It was over so quickly, I couldn't believe it. Was that all there was to it, I wondered. That was simple enough. Surely Chuck would be consoled how easily it had gone.

A bailiff got up and escorted Chuck out of the room. Several minutes later, Chuck returned and announced his probation officer was located in the courthouse, just across the street and he would have to go over there. He seemed cold and distant. Feeling uneasy, I moved away from him. We filed out of the hearing room and over to the courthouse, Chuck leading the way. Up on the ninth floor, he located the correct office and we followed him in. After making inquiries as to whom he was to see, he discovered his probation officer was a woman, Paulette Kaupanger. However, she wasn't there at the moment, and he would have to call later for an appointment or come back another time. To Chuck, this meant further delay, more frustration, no resolution. We stood looking at one another blankly. "Where do we go from here?"

Breaking the silence, Ron recommended we go to a restaurant for a cup of coffee. I was feeling scared and uncertain of where Chuck was emotionally. I welcomed the suggestion thinking, anything to avoid going home with him. On the main floor of the courthouse, we found a coffee shop and went in. It was crowded with courthouse employees on their break. The hostess approached Ron and asked the usual particulars, how many, smoking or non-smoking, and then led the way to a vacant table in the middle of the room, surrounded on all sides by people. We were seated so that Ron was across from Chuck, and Nancy at his side. Feeling endangered being near Chuck, I sat next to Ron.

It was noisy and this added to my tension, since whenever Chuck spoke, he had to speak loudly to be heard and his increased volume emphasized his anger.

The waitress arrived to take our order. Once she was gone, Chuck exploded. "I hope she's happy," letting out a sigh of exasperation.

Ron leaned forward, hoping to calm Chuck down by talking softly, asked, "What do you mean, Chuck? What's wrong?"

But, Chuck would not be calmed. Instead, he leaned back in his seat and in a clamorous voice responded, "Didn't you hear the judge? Now, I'll have to take another day off from my job for my sentencing. Plus coming back down to see this fucking probation officer."

Ron looked embarrassed and self-conscious. He

leaned even closer to Chuck, urging him to get control of himself. "Calm down Chuck, calm down."

But Chuck never heard him; he was off again. He leaned forward putting one of his arms on the table as he addressed Ron. "Did you see that judge? He never even once looked at me. What does he think I am, some kind of animal?"

"He sounded fair enough to me Chuck," came Ron's reply as the waitress approached with our order.

Chuck was oblivious of her presence and went on with resentment in his voice. "I feel emasculated. And to think I have to appear before him again. I won't go, do you hear? I won't do it."

His anger was obvious by now to all around us and people were staring. The waitress hesitated in her approach, so that Ron had to encourage her to come forward.

All this time, Nancy and I just sat there quietly, letting Ron handle Chuck. She had reached across the table and was holding my hand, trying to reassure me. As the waitress served us, Nancy took her hand back, but as soon as the woman was gone, Nancy's hand was there again.

Ron hung in there with Chuck, trying to be calm and encouraging. "You weren't charged with a felony, Chuck, only a misdemeanor."

"That's the only decent thing about this whole mess today." And then he continued to rant and rave about the judge, the hearing, the probation officer not being there, having to take off from work, etc. "I hope she's satisfied. I hope she's gotten what she wanted." He straightened up and hit the table with his fist, causing both the dishes and me to jump. "I want to just go off and kill myself."

Ron took his statement seriously. "Do we need to take you to a hospital, Chuck?"

Again he continued on without having heard Ron, "I

should have had a lawyer. I knew I should have had a lawyer."

With that, he withdrew into himself and was silent for a moment. Taking advantage of the lull, we drank our coffee and breathed easy for a moment.

By the time we were ready to leave, Chuck had his second wind and was starting in again. He was as angry as when we first arrived. Nancy and I had stepped into the lobby while Chuck and Ron took care of the bill. I was still having difficulty breathing and Nancy could tell I was feeling uneasy and scared. "Are you going to be all right, M'Liss?" she asked as we stood there.

My eyes welled with tears. "I feel threatened and afraid. He hasn't calmed down at all and I don't believe it's safe for me to go home with him. He's in the same frame of mind he was in last night."

Nancy handed me a kleenex. I dabbed at my eyes and blew my nose as I went on, "Did you see him, Nancy? He never looked at me once the whole time we sat there and everything he was saying to Ron was really for my benefit. I can't imagine what he is still so upset about—everything went just like we thought it would, just exactly as we were told. Except," I paused for emphasis, "the charge is a misdemeanor, thank God, and not a felony. I should think he'd be elated."

Nancy put an arm around me. "M'Liss, if you don't feel comfortable about going home with him, you don't have to. We'll work out some other arrangements."

Feeling more secure, I wiped my eyes again, just as the men were coming out of the restaurant.

"What's the matter with you?" Chuck asked curtly as though he were seeing me for the first time.

I moved a little closer to Nancy, but answered him as honestly as I could. "I'm feeling scared, Chuck, and I don't think I want to go home with you."

"Well, what do you propose then?" he barked again.

Nancy, feeling uncomfortable standing in the restaurant lobby with people going in and out, suggested we go outside and find some other place to resolve the problem.

Chuck was impatient with all of us. He snapped, "Well, my parking meter has expired and I need to go put some more money in it if we're going to stand around until she feels better."

Ron and Chuck left to take care of the cars while Nancy and I found a park bench across the street from the courthouse. We sat down to talk and I started to shake uncontrollably. "Last night, Chuck was just like this. He's so intense right now, I feel panicky."

Nancy reassured me again that I wouldn't have to go home with Chuck if I was hesitant in any way. We continued to wait for the men.

When they returned, I could tell immediately that Chuck wasn't in any better frame of mind. In fact, he started in again threatening suicide. Even Ron and Nancy began to feel more uneasy.

Chuck's impatience with me was growing by the minute. "It isn't worth it Ron, she isn't worth it. Take her with you, I'll go home by myself. I feel like excess baggage that no one knows what to do with." He closed his eyes for a moment and shook his head in self-abhorrence. "I'm tired of this and I'm tired of her. I'll just end it all and everyone can get on with life. You've already gone the extra mile with all you've done. I don't want to put you out any longer."

Nancy, who hadn't said anything to Chuck all this time, now spoke. "Chuck, I'm feeling really uncomfortable about you going home alone in this frame of mind. Would you consider going to a hospital?"

He shook his head. "Nancy, I'm not worth the trouble or expense. I wouldn't even consider it."

"Chuck, I agree with Nancy." Ron interjected, shifting his weight from one foot to the other in a manner that reflected his uneasiness. "Your talk about suicide scares me. I know you tried it once before, and if you won't go to a hospital, would you consider going to the office and spending the day with me? I don't want you alone."

"I can't, Ron," he cried as a look of agony crept across his face. "I can't put you out like that."

We continued to explore alternatives, from calling Domestic Abuse Project, to even having Chuck go to the police.

As he began to take in our genuine concern and care for him, he started to cry. "I don't really want to kill myself. I just feel so helpless, like a worthless piece of shit. I just don't know what to do." He paused, breathing softly, rhythmically. "I'm not going to hurt you, M'Liss. Come on, let's go home and let these people get on with their business. I've taken up enough of their day already."

He had started his descent. He was in so much terror of losing his job, so much insecurity from things being totally out of his control, so much pain from the embarrassment of being caught, he could scarcely bear it. "I just don't know what to do," he repeated, lifting his glasses to wipe his eyes. I'm all right, M'Liss, honest I am. I won't hurt you."

You could see it in his face, the de-escalation, his muscles relaxing, his hands unclenching. He was letting go.

I sensed it immediately, and my own shaking began to subside. "I'm feeling okay now, Nancy, about going home. I believe we'll be all right."

Nancy too could see the changes. Nevertheless, she wasn't that sure. "M'Liss, I don't want you to go unless you're absolutely sure. You know you're welcome to spend the day at our house. You don't have to go. Are you taking care of yourself, or us?" she questioned.

"Yes," I assured her, "I really believe it's okay and we can handle it."

Again, Nancy checked it out, wanting to be sure I wasn't giving in so Ron could go to work and she to her business. You could tell they were both hesitant to leave in spite of their need to get on with their own affairs.

"I'm okay now, Ron," said Chuck, taking up the cause. "We'll be all right."

Finally feeling convinced, Ron and Nancy prepared to leave. "Call if you need *anything*," demanded Ron. "You know where you can reach me."

"I will," Chuck told him as he reached out to take my hand.

As we headed for the car, I thought back over the last twelve hours. They had been a terrifying and intense nightmare, without a moment's let-up. I felt exhausted. In my wildest imaginings of Chuck's reaction to my charging him, I never dreamed it would be anything like it had been. Thank God I hadn't known. I might never have taken that first step.

We got in the car and drove quietly home. When we arrived, Chuck immediately called the courthouse and made an appointment to see his probation officer. He was able to schedule it for the next day which was his regular day off. He wouldn't have to request any more leave from work.

The next day at two in the afternoon, we were in Paulette Kaupanger's office for the investigation. She introduced herself in a gentle and soft-spoken voice. She helped us both to relax with her kind manner. The interrogation took approximately two hours. She questioned us about our different backgrounds, our children, Chuck's employment record, his abusive behavior. Then she asked Chuck if he had ever abused the children. He started to cry. "I love my kids," he replied, barely getting the words out. I felt moved with compassion. Paulette paused, giving him a moment to recover. Then going on, she asked his thoughts for a solution to

the abuse and he informed her of what he was already doing.

With that, the interview drew to a close. Paulette stood up. We followed. Looking eye to eye with Chuck, she told him that in view of the treatment he had committed himself to at Domestic Abuse Project, plus what he was already doing with the Men's Self-Help Group, she would recommend to the judge, "thirty to ninety days in jail and a two hundred and fifty dollar fine." She paused, letting it sink in, then went on. "In view of continued treatment, suspended to one year probation and a fifty dollar court fee." She hesitated again, then added. "You understand, this is only a suggestion to the court. The judge can do anything he wishes though he usually respects the recommendation of the investigators."

Chuck uttered his appreciation in a low weak voice. She arranged his sentencing to be on the following Friday, his day off. Again he was spared having to request more leave from his job.

We drove home feeling optimistic. And once more life took on some semblance of normality. After a relatively calm week, Friday at last rolled around.

We had decided to ask the children if they would like to come with us to the sentencing. We thought it would be a good way for them to be a part of what was happening. And it would give them an opportunity to support Chuck and to learn from the experience.

Ron met us for the second time at the Adult Detention Center. He told us Nancy had a work-related emergency and regretfully would not be able to be there. As we stood talking, Paulette arrived from the courthouse, offering her services to get Chuck's case presented among the first ones. She was aware that he had an appointment at Domestic Abuse Project for an interview and she was trying to accommodate him so he could make it on time.

Preceded by Paulette, we marched in and sat down. The proceedings began just as the week before. The children sat engrossed, watching the procession, as each offender made his pilgrimage to the bench. Very shortly, Chuck was called. His charge was repeated, and his plea stated. This time, the judge looked at him. He informed Chuck he could do anything he wanted, that he didn't have to go by the recommendation of the investigator. He went on to comment that in view of the fact that Chuck was already seeking help and would be starting treatment at Domestic Abuse Project, he would sentence him to sixty days in jail and a two hundred dollar fine.

The children gasped.

Then, pausing for effect, as Paulette had done, he continued. "Suspended to fifty dollars fine and one year probation." He proceeded to make it very clear that should Chuck at anytime during that year break his probation with another assault, the sentence would take immediate effect. The case was dismissed, and we all got up and filed out.

Everything had gone exactly as I had been told it would. The law had served its purpose. It had accomplished for me what I had been begging Chuck for years to do: to get help for himself. He had refused; the violence continued. He left me with no other choice but to use the system, to call him to account.

CHAPTER 10

Shortly after the actual trial was over, Chuck and I began our therapy at Domestic Abuse Project, DAP. Designed to address the specific problems we were dealing with, the program provides counseling sessions for men, women and children. Chuck and I met in separate groups twice a week for eight weeks for Phase I, then once a week for twenty weeks for Phase II. The children would begin the program after we finished Phase I. After Phase II, Chuck and I would be together in a Couples Group for ten weeks and finally, we would come together as a family for Family Group for eight weeks.

I arrived with high expectations. We couldn't get started soon enough to suit me. The women's group met in an upstairs room that served during the day as an office. We were seated in a circle on various kinds of chairs someone had collected for our purpose. The counselor arrived and introduced herself to us as Paula Poorman. We quickly went to work, first introducing ourselves and then establishing the rules for our interactions over the next few weeks. They included punctuality, confidentiality, no use of alcohol or drugs on meeting days, and honesty in reporting all violent incidents.

For the first few meetings, various "source" persons came to our group. They shared briefly information about the purpose of the children's program and legal services available to us through the court systems, and

an Order of Protection we could get to keep our husbands out of the house if necessary. This part was hard
for me to sit through. I was eager to begin. I had already
used the courts, I didn't need an Order of Protection. I
just wanted to get started. But, we had started and this
was all considered necessary information that we would
possibly need in the future.

What I enjoyed more from those beginning sessions
was the sharing time. We spent part of several weeks
listening to each one in the group tell her own story. I
was astonished listening to the stories of these women.
They had lived with the same fears and terrors I had experienced. The stories were different in details, but I was
amazed at how alike they all were basically.

Jodie's husband was an alcoholic. He abused her and
she passed it on to the children. The alcohol treatment
center had referred them to DAP.

Sarah's husband beat her often and the last time she
had called the police. He was arrested, and as a result of
that incident, she had learned about DAP. At this point
they were still living together, but so far he refused to attend DAP.

Diane was divorced. Her ex-husband had abused her
unmercifully. She was presently being counseled by a
therapist who thought she needed to be with other battered women. He believed it would help her understand
what had happened and prevent it from happening
again.

Alice too was divorced from the husband who abused
her. Engaged to be married, she had had a recent scare
when her ex-husband threatened to kill both her and her
fiance. She was at DAP to learn to avoid the possibility
of future abuse from either her former or future husband. One incident she shared with us reflected what I
believe to be the superficial attitude people sometimes
seem to have toward abuse. Alice had been hospitalized
following a violent incident. Her head had a bad cut and

required stitches. An intern came by and jokingly asked, "What happened? Did your husband beat you up?" He laughed, and went on without an answer. Her embarrassment lasted a long time.

Linda had been abused by her husband even before they were married. She now had a baby boy and was concerned that her own strong temper, coupled with the abuse she had suffered, might lead to her abuse of her child. She wanted to prevent that.

Kathy was from the Phillipines. She had met her husband as a result of a "pen pal" relationship. He went to the Phillipines, married her and brought her back to the States. He beat her from the very start of their marriage. She wanted to go back home but had no money. Although Kathy worked, her husband took all her money. Now she was pregnant and scared. She came to DAP because the court had referred her husband there after a particularly savage beating.

Perhaps the most interesting of all was Marcy. She had been ordered to participate in DAP after she had attempted to have her husband murdered. Marcy was currently waiting to stand trial and needed support and help. Her husband had beaten her many times—several times seriously enough for her to be hospitalized. Now, she thought he was going to kill her.

The thing that I noted about all these women was that they were younger than I and had been married relatively short periods of time. Yet here they were involved in a program that had taken me twenty years to get to. Why had I stayed so long? Why didn't I do something before?

When it came my turn to share, I told them my story and related also the observations I had noted after hearing them talk. Paula pointed out that for many years there was no help available to women in violent relationships. Thinking through my background, I began to realize that it wasn't only my religious beliefs and my sense of responsibility that had bound me to the situation with Chuck. With him, there was always an apology, a demonstration of love after the abuse, something I had never gotten from my oldest sister. Life with Chuck was better than anything I had ever known. I also reminded myself of our effort to work with a psychiatrist ten years earlier. I felt confident that if DAP had existed earlier and if I had been aware of it, I would have been there.

As we talked and shared among ourselves in group, one commonality emerged. We all believed we were responsible for the violence. "If I hadn't said that." "If I had been on time." "If I hadn't forgotten the ketchup on the picnic, I would not have been hit." It was the same for all the women in the group. We accuse ourselves, our husbands blame us, society condemns us. As unreasonable as it seems, abused women are denounced as the ones responsible for the violence by themselves, by their husbands and by society.

So Paula went to work to dispel the myth, to deprogram our thinking. She reassured us that there was nothing that could occur between two people to justify violence except self-defense. She impressed on us that it was our husbands' choice whether to hit or not. No action of ours made them do it. I knew what she was saying was true. It was common sense, but I had accepted the blame for so long, her words felt contrary to my thinking. I had actually believed Chuck had a right and was justified in hitting me. I felt so excited listening to all of this, I could hardly contain myself. I was like a dry thirsty sponge just soaking it all in.

About four weeks into Phase I, Paula explained for us the cycle of violence. I sat with my mouth open in wonder as I listened. What she was telling us fit Chuck's and my behavior to a tee. The cycle, she said, was first defined by Lenore E. Walker in her book *The Battered Woman.* It has three stages. The first, the tension-building stage, can last a few hours, days, months, and even years. There are minor incidents that arouse his displeasure. He makes his dissatisfaction known by degrading her, hollering, slamming a door, throwing objects, or destroying property. With each new occurrence, the tension builds. During this time, the woman tries everything she knows to calm him down. Finally, the tension can go no higher. She has failed to calm him, it is her own fault, she didn't do it right or well enough. Something happens, significant or insignificant, and the second stage begins. To bring things back into his control, she is beaten. This could mean a shove, being restrained, or hit with an object, a slap or punch, being kicked or strangled, whatever it takes to appease his anger. This goes on until she has learned the lesson, or he is too tired to hit anymore. If she resists, he may become worse. Having vented his anger, he becomes calm again, rational, reasonable, and the third stage begins. Some men go on to apologize while others may not. But life has returned to what it had been for her in the beginning. She then decides she can live with this. Then, before she knows it, the cycle has started again, and the tension has begun to build.

Yet for some of the women in the group, this was not the case. One woman expressed that her husband never said he was sorry. To her it seemed like he never became peaceful or calm either. Rather, she said, he moved right back into the first phase, the tension just starting immediately to build again.

Some in the group told how their husbands would buy them things after the abuse. Or they were just generally more cooperative with everything.

At some point during all of this, I confessed that I thought I sometimes instigated Chuck's violence. Paula explained that some women, sensing the period of inevitability is very close, and unable to tolerate the terror or anxiety any longer, will occasionally provoke the explosion. I could relate to that experience and hearing Paula's explanation helped relieve some of my guilt.

She went on to say that the woman learns to withdraw or protect herself emotionally from acknowledging physical danger by denying he's upset. Or, she may tell herself he's just had a bad day, or he's really mad at someone else. She protects herself by catering to him or fixing him something to eat. She minimizes the danger or rationalizes his behavior. She may even fantasize about it. In the sexual aspect, she again gives in, or caters to him at her own expense.

The payoff of this withdrawal is that she is able to cope with what is happening. She doesn't feel the pain and it gives her reason to stay. It keeps her from having to tell someone and from being humiliated. But the negative consequences are the loss of her self-esteem and the denial of her own feelings and anger. It was all part of the ongoing cycle we were all caught up in.

Once we understood the cycle of violence, Paula asked us to identify the cues that told us the escalation process was beginning. What did we sense about our husbands that warned us of the approaching danger? We all responded. Some said their husbands became "moody," others said "crabby," I listed "impatient." The inventory went on and on: "not listening, name-calling, withdrawing affection, uncooperative." We were all surprised at the similarities.

Next, we listed our cues, what we noticed about ourselves that indicated things were escalating. This was harder. Paula got us started by asking if we did anything when we sensed the tension building. I responded, "I fix Chuck something to eat." "I ask how he feels," said someone else. "Usually, when he tells me how he feels, I can better decide how to take care of him, to calm him down. If he says he's tired, I suggest he take a nap and I'll keep the children quiet and out of the way for him.

Or, if he is bored, I'll turn on the T.V. for him and in this way divert his attention."

"I feel like I'm walking on eggs," added Linda. Another felt tight inside, another scared. I volunteered that I sometimes would have company over in hopes of distracting Chuck. Alice noted that she would do nothing. She remarked that she would just sit down and stare ahead, seeing nothing.

Next, we focused on the earliest sign for each of us that told us our husbands' tension levels were escalating. For me, my chest would get tight. Also, my listening and observation senses were more alert.

Now we were ready to learn what to do when we noticed these signs. Paula taught us to ask for a simple "time out." When we perceive that our husbands are moody, impatient, under pressure, and we are feeling scared, tense, nervous, or we start staring ahead, it's the moment to call a "time out." At this point, the escalation has not advanced high enough for an explosion and it is still calm enough to get away. This "time out" must be done way back at the beginning while everyone is still fairly calm and under control.

My mistake in the past had been to try to escape when the level of escalation was too advanced and Chuck would anticipate my leaving and block the way. I could readily see that this new system for getting away for a break might really be possible.

So it was important for each of us to work out our own individual protection plan. Paula helped us look at what we could do the next time we saw our husbands' tension levels escalating, where we could go, what options were available to us. For each one that plan could be different, but we gained ideas from each other as we brainstormed.

I was learning so much, so fast; the weeks were flying by. To give me more opportunity to explore individually the things I was learning in group, I began to meet with Joanne Kittel, my individual therapist. She would also be our Phase II leader. One thing that interested me was the definition of sexual abuse. I had a growing belief that I had experienced that with Chuck. There had been times in our relationship when I felt compelled by fear to have sexual intercourse though I didn't want to. There were also times when Chuck, having been angry and abusive to me, would want to make up by having intercourse. I realized that often times he would use sex to reassure himself that I had forgiven him and everything was okay between us. It was a form of security to him. Joanne and I discussed these things and she encouraged me to trust my intuition and call for a "time out" the next occasion I had reservations about having intercourse.

We also discussed Chuck's dependency on me and how I "care-take" him. Care-take in my case meant I determined Chuck's needs often before he was aware of them, and I'd jump to meet them. I shielded him from all the children's questions, needs, discipline, and took care of them myself. If he got involved, I feared something would be said or done that could set him off. If something needed fixing, it was safer for me to do it than to ask him. When he was home, I tried to keep things quiet and out of his way. I planned all our outings and I read the maps. By handling everything myself, I could better control the number of mistakes and thus reduce the incidents that caused escalation. If something went wrong then, it was my own fault. No one else was to blame.

Joanne showed me in black and white what my relationship to Chuck looked like. I had assumed the role of parent, a major part of my personality. She went on to explain that this was only natural for me, since I had always met everyone's needs except my own after the death of my parents. It was a warped version of "love your neighbor as yourself." Coupled with my childhood and religious training, it was only natural that I "take care" of my husband.

Chuck, on the other hand, needed lots of caring for. He operated largely from his "child" perspective. He had been convinced as a boy that he couldn't care for himself. So in our marriage relationship, as the years went by, I became more responsible for him and he less accountable for himself. He spent his time hiding in the television and sleeping. He never fed the babies or changed a diaper. He never did the dishes, vacuumed, or changed the bed. He rarely fixed anything. Joanne went on to show me how my "care-taking" was getting me in trouble. Because I assumed his responsibilities, then I naturally would receive the rebuke when I didn't do them right. I was denying Chuck his share in the rearing of our children whether he wanted it or not. I was protecting him from himself. He feared failure, making a mistake, taking a risk. As long as I would do these things for him, he would never grow, or change. Did I want to carry all that load?

Meanwhile, the men's group was involved in learning some of the same concepts. They were being given much of the same information. The advocates had spoken to them at the beginning as they had to the women. They too had shared with each other their own stories. Some of them were husbands to the women in my group.

They explored and discussed the issue: why men batter. Their leader shared with them a brief profile of the origin, process, and personality of an abuser. He told them that research had revealed that for most of the abusers, it was a learned behavior as well as influenced by culture. Many saw their parents fight a lot. That same anger was turned on them by one or both parents. At first they knew it wasn't right, but as they got older, they adapted to their situation, thinking most families beat each other. They learned to express their frustrations this way, hitting on the playground and on the athletic field. The macho image men are supposed to portray adds to it. Boys don't cry, do dishes, play with dolls, etc. Eventually they get married. According to tradition their wife is supposed to be submissive. But she does something they don't approve of and they get angry. They try to keep their feelings to themselves, but other frustrations pile up on top of the anger until they can't hold it in anymore. He went on to explain that while they appear agreeable to the outside world, inside they feel anger, frustration, insecurity, and despair building up, creating stress that's never released. They aren't aware of the buildup. They seem to function well in society and in low-stress situations. They are compliant, not very assertive. They swallow and swallow and swallow—then they don't swallow anymore. It is an either/or thing for them. They opt to deal with stress in the way their parents taught them. They believe that they explode in response to a particular incident, when in fact they do so to regain control and to expel all the accumulated stress.

This description the leader gave fit each man in the group in one way or another. It served as a bridge, filling in the gulf of guilt that stood before them. Though the choice to be abusive was theirs alone, this history helped provide an understanding for why they made that choice.

During this initial phase of Chuck's therapy he was angry and resentful. He focused on other people as the cause of his pain, rather than his own behavior. He blamed me, DAP, his counselor, and the whole order of things for what was happening to him. He experienced so much pressure to change from these sources, that he felt out of control, like shooting the rapids of a river without any previous experience. He tried to get back some control and bend things in his direction by being compliant to everything he was told to do, whether he understood or agreed with it or not. He felt like a criminal and viewed his therapist as his prison guard. He thought if he wasn't compliant, he would be thrown out of the program. He didn't understand what was going on or what they were trying to do. He felt like he had been stuffed into a grain hopper and with the turning of the crank a new person was being extruded through the sharp cutting blades that tore him every way but loose. He wanted a simple solution, a few quick answers to his problems. But as time went on, he began to realize this was going to be a long, drawn out and painful procedure. With this realization, he yielded himself to the process of putting one foot in front of the other and confusedly pressed forward.

Over time most of the men began to accept the responsibility for their violence. That was the hardest admission for them to make, but the beginning of their healing. By denying responsibility for their actions, they would never have to do anything about them. They learned that they too minimized the seriousness of their abuse and by so doing ignored the danger.

The men were taught the same concept of the "time outs" and encouraged to use them. They also looked at their own body and sensory cues that signaled to them the buildup of tension. Some of these cues were feeling tense, raising their voice, being impatient, thinking negative thoughts, and fantasizing. They practiced assertiveness and learned other methods for releasing and coping with tension so as to reduce the level of stress.

They learned to identify and express their feelings without feeling threatened. For most of them when they began, the only feeling they acknowledged was anger. Now they were learning that often their anger was a cover-up for feeling hurt, confused, inadequate or afraid. By putting a more accurate word to the feeling, they often found the feeling less threatening.

Things were really moving along for Chuck and me.

We were using our "time outs" with positive effects, and the violence seemed a thing of the past. The potential was exciting, the hope renewing. I thought we were really on our way.

CHAPTER 11

However, my optimism was short-lived. Toward the end of Phase I, an incident occurred that caused me to question our progress.

We were experiencing some turbulence arising from two areas. First, our relationship with our church was deteriorating. Our friends there seemed embarrassed by our problem and kept their distance. The sermons continued to address "lost sinners" rather than "troubled saints." Our impression was that our church was made up of perfect people and we didn't fit in. We felt like black sheep. We had serious problems, and no one wanted anything to do with us.

Secondly, we learned that Chuck was going to have to make a trip to Oklahoma for some job-related training. He would be gone a week and miss two DAP sessions. We both felt anxious about that, and I was always uneasy when Chuck was away.

So it probably shouldn't have surprised either of us that a blow-up was building.

It began as we were heading home from DAP one Thursday evening. Chuck was driving and we were discussing something that had come up in my group. The conversation became heated and I asked for a "time out." We stopped talking for a few minutes. When we resumed the conversation, it again became heated and this time Chuck asked for "time out." As he did, he pulled the car over and got out, walking away without a word. One of the rules for "time out" is that you state how long it's for, and if you leave, when you'll be back. Chuck's behavior left me feeling confused and insecure. I didn't know if he was coming back or if I should go on home without him. I called after him and he came back. I reminded him of the rules for "time out" and he felt caught. He had made a mistake, and now he became defensive, then blaming, then feeling frustrated saying we needed to write down the rules.

"Chuck, all I need to know is should I wait for you to return or are you walking home from here?"

He opened his door and got into the car. I felt tense. What was he going to do? I couldn't tell how upset he was. He started the car and we continued on home without another word.

When we got home, we sat down at the table and talked a little about the "time out" rules. Chuck agreed that it would have been best for him to have told me what he intended. Then we again started on the subject that had caused the escalation in the first place. It was still too sensitive for us, so we went on to bed. I felt a little tense and unresolved and I sensed Chuck was feeling insecure. I believed with time, we could work our differences out. We got into bed and Chuck started kissing me more passionately than the usual good-night kiss. I realized he wanted sex. But I also believed that because of my own feelings, this was one of those times when I didn't feel okay about it. My intuition was telling me something wasn't right. I believed that he was wanting to use our sexual intercourse to reassure himself that everything was okay between us. I kissed him and took his hands in mine. "Chuck," I began, feeling hesitant to do something I had never done before, "I don't feel okay about having sex tonight while we are still unresolved. I would like a 'time out' from sex until this other matter is settled."

He was shocked at first. Then he replied, "All right, if that's what you want," and he rolled over. I settled in to sleep too. Moments passed, he rolled back and asked me if that meant that I was going to start "cutting him off" now. I told him no, and tried to reassure him that I just didn't feel good about it right now. He sounded scared as he responded with "okay," then, rolled back to his side of the bed. A few more minutes passed. Then the next thing I knew he was sitting on me pinning my arms to the bed. "I'd like to kill you right now." He breathed heavily as he went on. "Is this the beginning of a long line of refusals? I can go elsewhere you know."

"Chuck, please don't do this," I begged, "I only want a time out because I don't feel good about sex right now. I sense you're feeling insecure and I believe you use our sex sometimes to take that feeling away." I continued to try to make him understand, but I held firm in my position. "I don't want our sexual relationship to be used for that. I love you and we can work this out, but not with sex. You'll just have to trust me and our relationship, because I refuse to have intercourse anymore when I don't feel peaceful about it. Something is wrong. It isn't anything we can't handle, but sex isn't the answer to fixing it right now. Sex won't fix it, at least not for me and in reality it's a false fix for you. Please don't do anything you'll regret Chuck, please."

He sat there for a moment more, the veins in his neck standing out against his skin. Then he slowly got off of me. "I've gone too far already," he said as he stood beside the bed. "We're not going to make it. I just know we're not going to make it." Sounding dejected, defeated, and lost, he walked around to the other side and got back in. He lay there quietly for a long time. I scarcely breathed. At last he spoke, "I'm okay M'Liss. Do what you need to do. I have no choice but to trust you, I guess."

I slept lightly. Chuck tossed and turned a lot too. In

the morning, I called DAP and reported the incident as was agreed when I signed up. They connected me to a counselor and she took down the information, questioning me about how I was feeling, if I thought I was safe and if I needed anything. I told her I was sure I was safe, minimizing as in the past, the danger I had been in.

Chuck had a four o'clock appointment that day with his primary counselor, Mark Raderstorf, and he reported the incident to him. Mark told him that if he wanted to continue in the program, he would have to find another place to live and move out of the house.

When Chuck came home and told me this, I felt resigned. I was ready for him to go. I was no longer frightened by the thought of his being gone. I was determined that I was going to change, and I could survive without him if I had to. I was no longer going to put up with taking the blame or being hurt. I was prepared to pay whatever the cost to do this, even if it meant the end of our marriage.

We spent the next two days looking for an apartment. Two miles from our house, we found an efficiency apartment, with a small stove and refrigerator, and a little wash basin for a sink. It also had a dresser, bed, table and two chairs. There was a stained striped carpet on the floor and a toilet in the closet. The showers were down the hall. The table was about seventy years old, the chairs about fifty. The bed sagged badly and there were bugs in the cupboards. But it would serve the purpose and we agreed to take it. Chuck said he would move in when he returned from Oklahoma.

I took him to the airport on Sunday. I felt anxious about him missing DAP at this point, but there was nothing we could do about it.

On Tuesday, I went to my group, prepared to share the incident of Thursday night and our decision about his moving out. While I was concerned over the incident, I felt good about our response to it. I had reported it and Chuck was moving out. My DAP group would be satisfied with my actions and supportive of our decision.

I thought back a few weeks, when Kathy had shown up with her face bruised and cut. She told us that her husband had thrown a coffee cup at her after she had spilled some. It had upset her, and with her pregnancy, made her nauseous. She had grabbed an ice cream bucket and began vomiting into it. Her husband, still angry, shoved her head down into the bucket, cutting and bruising her face. We all had sympathized with her, and tried to encourage her to consider taking out an Order of Protection, but she had refused saying she couldn't support herself or even get to her place of employment without his help. Remembering this, I felt satisfied that I could report that we had made arrangements for Chuck to move out.

So, with Chuck in Oklahoma, I headed for DAP. As I reported the incident to the group, and our handling of it, I sensed an expectancy among them. When I finished, Paula spoke. "What are you going to do about it, M'Liss?"

I stared blankly at her. "We've already done it. We moved Chuck out." I replied, looking around for support. Seeing silent faces looking back at me, I asked in a puzzled voice, "What else should I do?"

The answer came almost in unison. "Take out an Order of Protection."

I recoiled in shock. "What for?" I felt hurt and defensive. "There's no reason to do that. Chuck is out of the house and I don't think we'll have any more problems."

Paula asked quickly, "Haven't we heard that before from you, M'Liss?"

That stung. I felt embarrassed, caught. I had made the statement the night I told "my story" that I didn't think Chuck would ever do anything to hurt me again.

He was so scared and shook up about being charged in the first place I was confident he would never jeopardize himself again. Yet it had happened. I was standing face to face with the fact that the charge wasn't enough. He had willfully violated his probation, in spite of all his fears. He had been abusive again.

"Did he report the incident to his probation officer?" Paula continued to probe.

"No," I weakly answered, looking down at the floor.

"Have you reported it?"

Again I responded, "No."

Paula persisted with her investigation, each of her questions hitting its mark as accurately as an arrow on a bullseye. "Are you protecting him, M'Liss? Are you still taking care of Chuck?"

Tears came to my eyes. It was true. I wanted to get by with taking less than full responsibility for my safety. I didn't want to do anything to cause further inconvenience or trouble for him.

Diane spoke to me gently, with tenderness in her voice. "M'Liss, I'm scared for you. I believe you need to take out an Order of Protection."

Linda joined in. "You know, M'Liss, just having Chuck out of the house doesn't mean you're safe. He could come back anytime he feels like it and you won't be able to do a thing about it. I thought you were committed to going all the way, M'Liss. I thought you made that decision when you first charged Chuck."

More of the same from Alice. "I'm scared for you too. You've said before he wouldn't abuse you again. You were so confident. Now he's said he wants to kill you, and you're not worried about it?" She took a deep breath. "Think, M'Liss."

What struck me about all this input was that I was hearing back the same things I had said to them when they reported incidents of violence. I could see their danger; I could feel fear for them. Yet, because it was my husband, someone familiar to me, I wasn't feeling the same concern. I was minimizing again. I was also projecting that such an action could hurt our relationship, maybe lead to divorce. Was I ready to go that far?

But as I considered their arguments, I knew they were right. I had made my decision when I first had Chuck charged. The Order of Protection was merely a follow-through of a strategy already undertaken. I couldn't make it work with a half-hearted commitment. I needed to make up my mind to start running in earnest, or else get out of the race.

With tears flowing down my cheeks, I looked around, from face to face. I knew I wasn't just letting myself and Chuck down, I was letting them down too. "You're right," I relented. "I have to do it. It's the right thing to do. Chuck broke his probation and he'll have to be responsible for that. I don't want to protect or take care of him any longer."

There was silence, but this time I could feel the approval, the encouragement, and the support.

CHAPTER 12

As I was driving home that night, I acknowledged to myself what I would have to do. Charging Chuck in the first place had felt like I was betraying him, much as God must have felt, giving up Jesus to the angry mob. It was like I was giving him up to be crucified. Then, when my friend betrayed me by sharing our problem with someone we had chosen not to share it with, I felt betrayal again. I had my Judas. And now I was having to discipline Chuck a second time. I would have to take out an order that would remove his right to come to his own home. He would be on his own. Again, I related to God and how He must have felt turning His back on Jesus at the cross. I would be turning my back on Chuck. I felt the pain and started to cry. I knew I had to do it. Jesus once said, "No one builds a structure without first counting the cost to see if he can afford to complete what he starts." Or, "No one goes to war without first seeing that he can in fact beat the enemy. Otherwise, he goes and makes peace while the enemy is still afar off." I had started to build when I charged Chuck. Was I willing to pay the price, to see it to its end? The price was so high, so terribly distressing, bitter, unendurable. Perhaps I should make peace with the enemy and give up all I had gained. But, I saw that price as even higher. I continued to sob uncontrollably. Why did I always have to be the one to take the initiative? I felt resentful. Why did I have to be the strong one? My heart felt heavy under the burden. I knew I had to do it if I wanted to see this to the end. Gritting my teeth, I "set my face toward Jerusalem." I felt God's ministering angel comfort me and give me courage.

Thus resolved, I pulled into the garage and went to the house. It was good timing on God's part, because as I entered, the phone was ringing. It was Chuck, calling from Oklahoma. He sounded in a good mood and anxious to be able to talk to me.

"M'Liss," he inquired, sounding casual and relaxed, "how was your session tonight? Are you doing all right?"

I mumbled something ambiguous.

He went on talking, telling me about the people he was working with and what he was learning.

After a few minutes, there was a pause. Gathering together my determination and courage, I took advantage of it to say what needed to be said.

"Chuck, I think your probation officer needs to know about last Thursday's incident. I plan to call her tomorrow and I'm also going to take out an Order of Protection."

The phone clicked, the line went dead and our connection was broken. I looked blankly at the receiver in my hand, then pressed the button two or three times trying to reestablish contact. Failing, I thought Chuck must have hung up on me. A queasy feeling crept over me as the likelihood of that possibility set in. Chuck could be out of control. Even a thousand miles away from him, I felt vulnerable and helplessly afraid. What was he doing? What if he tried to commit suicide again? That thought was unbearable. It was more than I could endure. I took the phone off the hook so he couldn't call and threaten me with that. I sat there a few minutes, gaping at the receiver. Chuck might need to call for help —I couldn't just leave him like that. I put the receiver back. I stared a few more minutes and decided that maybe what he would do would be to try to make a deal —no suicide attempt if I wouldn't call his probation officer. I took the receiver back off. A few minutes after this decision, I began to realize that I was probably the one out of control, and I needed help. Taking up the phone again, I called the DAP hotline. Fortunately, a good counselor was available. Over the next few minutes, he helped me work through my feelings and fears for Chuck. He assisted me in realizing Chuck had some help available to him there. If Chuck threatened suicide, I could encourage him to call an Oklahoma hotline, or some friends of ours who lived there at the time. And, if I became too scared or upset talking to Chuck, he assured me I could always hang up myself. I began to feel strong. My direction became clear again, my thinking sound.

I hung up the phone.

A few minutes later, it rang again.

Picking it up, I heard Chuck's voice. His tone was even, controlled. "M'Liss, we got cut off. That was my fault. I'm sorry. I was calling from a pay phone and didn't have enough money for more than three minutes. I had to get some more money to call back."

I could have cried with relief. He hadn't hung up on me at all!

Going on, he asked quietly, "M'Liss, I need you to go on. Please tell me the rest."

"Chuck, I don't know what else to tell you," I answered, gripping the receiver tightly, "except to repeat what I have already said. I am going to call your probation officer tomorrow, and I am serious about the Order of Protection."

I held my breath. Surely, now he would explode.

But, Chuck's voice came across the line, still bridled and easy. "I know I'm cutting my own throat, but you're right." He sounded defenseless, resigned. "I support you, M'Liss. What else can I say?"

I started crying then, and poured it all out. "Oh, Chuck," I wept, "I thought you had hung up on me. I thought you were going to kill yourself. Instead, I'm hearing you're going to back me up." Trying to control my sobs, I continued, "I can't believe my ears."

My breaking down alarmed Chuck. I could hear the concern and fear in his voice as he tried to reassure me. "M'Liss, I want to change. You know I want to stop hurting you. If that's what it takes to make me do it, I support you." He sounded determined.

It was this side of Chuck that caused me to continue to love him through the years. There was so much goodness there, so much potential. It had always been there and each time it surfaced, my hope in him was restored.

He had really been self-sacrificing in this interaction with me, and I wanted to give back to him. "Chuck," I suggested, "why don't you call and tell Paulette what happened? If you report the incident yourself, it might make a difference."

He seemed eager to take my offer. "I'd like to do that, if you'll give me the opportunity."

Noticing for the first time, my hand cramping from holding the receiver so tightly, I released my grip slightly. Still crying softly, and nodding my head, I encouraged him. "Chuck, I'll wait until ten thirty tomorrow morning to call your probation officer. That should give you plenty of time to call her first."

"I'll do it first thing in the morning," he rejoined, "and thanks."

I hung up the phone, trembling. My own fears had nearly done me in. I was convinced that the Order of Protection was another step in making Chuck take responsibility for his own actions, and yet it did seem that maybe I was pushing him pretty hard. I was relenting, weakening. When I was with the group at DAP, my resolve was firm. But now, by myself again, my fear of pushing Chuck over the brink, "forcing" him into depression, maybe even into suicide, made me hesitate.

Yet I reminded myself it was Chuck who was forcing these situations. I was not responsible. And if he decided to choose drastic options over the more reasonable ones of help and therapy, it was his own choice. Shoring myself up with these thoughts, I resolved once again to go ahead with the Order of Protection. Feeling confident and at peace with my decision, I appreciated all the more the principles I had learned at DAP. A lot had been accomplished. I had won another round with myself.

When I called Paulette the next day, she told me that Chuck had called her earlier. I felt relieved. Pressing on, I filed for the Order of Protection. To do this, I had to go to the courthouse and fill out some forms. Then I was required to take them to the Sheriff's office in the Adult Detention Center. (I was getting to know my way around.) Everyone was cooperative. When I arrived at the sheriff's office, they took the forms and told me they would serve the papers as soon as Chuck returned. Then in two weeks, we would have to appear in court. At that time, Chuck would be given an opportunity to contest the order. If he didn't attend the hearing, the judge would grant the order as stated for a period of one year. Meanwhile, until the hearing, it would be temporarily honored.

My actions felt harsh, yet, I believed I was consistently making strides in taking charge of my own life. My self-confidence was growing.

At the next DAP session, I reported all that had happened, all I had done. The reaction was praise and encouragement. That really felt good. Joanne informed me weeks later that many on the staff had marveled at my determination and strength.

Next, I concentrated on Chuck's upcoming move to the apartment. It signaled the very real possibility that the price I would have to pay for freedom from abuse included the breakup of my marriage. This was hard for me to deal with. Maybe Chuck wouldn't change. Maybe I would lose my marriage. So the days spent preparing for his move also included my gradual acceptance of that possible price. While it was more than I had ever bargained for, I was willing to pay it, if necessary. Also, with this realization that he might not change and that divorce was all that was left, I came to accept divorce as an option. My religious indoctrinations were breaking down under the reality of life. I could no longer accept the belief that I must stay at all costs, as some of my fellow church members had been telling me for years.

With the children's help, I took advantage of the time Chuck was in Oklahoma. We set to work getting his apartment ready. Their first reaction when they saw it was appalled disbelief. "Is this where Dad has to live? This is awful." Yet, they could see it come to life as we put some of "home" there, and they started feeling better and better about it as we turned that old dirty room upside down and transformed it into something liveable. We cleaned it up, stocked the cupboards with food, and brought in some pots, pans, and dishes. We hung some pictures on the walls, a curtain on the window, and towels on the hooks. This was good exposure for them. Someday they would be leaving home to live in dorms, apartments or their own homes. This experience would help take away some of that apprehension, fear of what they hadn't experienced. It wasn't all negative.

It was time for Chuck to return. Faithful in their support, Ron and Nancy agreed to come by when Chuck arrived. He packed up his clothes and the four of us went with him to his apartment. Working together, we helped him unload and then waited as he looked around his new quarters. As he peeked into his cupboards and recognized some of the things from home, his face relaxed and he looked more confident. After that, we all went out for a bite to eat and to allow Chuck some time to come to grips with and to express his fears and reservations about being on his own. Ron and Nancy gave him support and encouragement, expressing their belief that he could do it, that he could handle it. By the time I dropped him off that night, he was feeling strong and determined.

He wouldn't have to wait long to test his confidence. Chuck would have to work the next day. He would have to get himself up, get his own breakfast, pack his own lunch, and get out to the bus stop on time. All these things had been done for him for years. He had come to expect them.

I was determined not to worry about him.

Although much of it was very difficult for him, he managed to get to work on time by skipping breakfast. When he called home, I tried to sound interested and encouraging without interfering or taking responsibility off him.

As for me, I was beginning to enjoy the quietness of my home with Chuck gone. Free from having to worry about his needs, I relaxed. I was amazed at the effect his being gone had on me, and I became fully aware for the first time just how much of my energies went into focusing on his needs. Being detached to think about myself was a new experience for me. It felt refreshing. I had needed space from Chuck so badly and never realized it. Now that I had it, it was like taking a long stretch after being cramped in a small space for a long long time.

With Chuck gone from the house, me busy with DAP and my own issues of growth and change, the children were making the most of the opportunity. I discovered that Chuck's absence was an adjustment for them, too, and they were finding their own way of expressing it. Their jobs were being neglected. They were going off without leaving notes saying where they were or when they would be back. Things were disappearing and not being returned. So, I informed them we would be holding a family council meeting once a week to discuss any problems we had with one another and the weekly calendar of events. I was greeted with strong opposition and no cooperation. They complained they were being picked on and I was never home. So I tried to make the purpose of the meeting clear. I told them I would inform them of my plans and schedule and they could tell me theirs. I would bring up any issues with them and clearly state my expectations. Once the guidelines were clear, they seemed more enthusiastic, less threatened.

As we met week by week, I noticed their cooperation improving. During the week, I would list the things that weren't getting done. Then they would come peek at my list, and rush to do their chores before the next Sunday meeting. That was really satisfying. Discussing the calendar each week helped clarify everyone's activities so we could plan better. Each had the opportunity to be heard regarding what she or he wanted to see accomplished. I also used the council meeting to introduce the idea of their attending DAP. The response was, "That's okay for Mom and Dad, but don't expect us to go." Well, that had to be worked out too and the council meeting provided the opportunity for accomplishing it.

Meanwhile, the days passed. Chuck and I continued to meet with our respective DAP groups. He was feeling more and more confident with being on his own and his men's group gave him encouragement and support. Besides being accountable for his violence, he was working on breaking down his isolation, learning how to get support and nurturing from friends rather than depending entirely on me. And he was learning how the violence affected his own self-esteem and his attitude toward me.

He was also wrestling with the trauma of waiting to hear the consequences for his violation of the probation agreement. We learned from Paulette that there was a possibility Chuck might have to go back to court and face some jail time. So even while he was being helped through his group at DAP, he was under constant pressure. In addition, Chuck was feeling very alone in the apartment, detached from me and the children. We talked each day on the phone, and I tried to keep him posted on all the family activities. Nevertheless, he was unhappy with his noisy neighbors, his uncomfortable bed, and many other problems related to his separation from us. But at least I wasn't the one to have to deal with it. The conditions were ideal for him to learn how to take care of himself and how to use his group.

The hearing for the Order of Protection came. Chuck chose not to take off from work to appear. It was automatically granted. Meanwhile, I continued enjoying the freedom from the stressful situations Chuck was struggling with. Remembering his fears of jail from months earlier helped me feel better and better about the Order of Protection, and the whole situation in general. But while I was feeling better, Chuck was feeling worse. We were nearing the end of Phase I of our treatment, and while I was pleased with my own accomplishments in relinquishing the blame and responsibility, Chuck's struggle was intensifying. He was getting plenty of opportunities to practice taking care of himself. But like a child learning to walk, he was unsteady and unsure of himself. It was scary and each setback he experienced was painful. Yet he hung in there and fought for his life and for all he loved: his wife, his children, his home, and his beliefs.

CHAPTER 13

An important aspect in my recovery as a victim of abuse was to get in touch with my long suppressed feelings of anger. One of the objectives of Phase II at DAP was to help each of us acknowledge our anger and learn healthy ways to express it. One evening, Joanne asked each of us in my women's group to draw a picture of our anger, what we did with it, how we felt about it.

The results were revealing. One woman drew a stick of dynamite that had no fuse or means of exploding. Her anger was all penned in, with no way of discharging. Another drew a face with a gag drawn over her mouth. She was angry, but there was no safe place to talk about it. I drew a face with hands over the mouth symbolizing the same thing. Another drew a fetus that was being attacked by poisonous snakes. She felt like a helpless infant, vulnerable to venomous assault and there was no escape. The underlying message in all the pictures was the same. There was no place for any of us to express our anger. In following through with this exercise, Joanne suggested we each write a letter over the weekend to someone with whom we were really angry. We would not be mailing the letters necessarily, so we could say anything we wanted, any way we wished.

I sat there contemplating the assignment. Who did I feel angry with? Who did I want to write to? My thoughts didn't go to Chuck as I would have expected.

Instead, they went to my oldest sister, the one who had raised me after the death of my mother. I sat in disbelief. Why her? Why not Chuck? That was twenty years ago. Yet as I reflected on this, I realized that after every abusive incident with Chuck, we were able to resolve the issue once he became rational again. And, he would always apologize. My sister never had. She never acknowledged being abusive, let alone apologized for it. As far as I was concerned, I was the sole individual who considered her treatment of me to be cruel, malicious, and unkind. Part of me therefore doubted that my impression was accurate. Did it really happen that way, was it all that bad, was I crazy and her behavior acceptable and sane? I realized I had been unresolved about it all these years. I had repressed my feelings, my doubts, my resentment, my anger.

When I got home and found the time to sit down alone to write, I realized again that it was my sister I wanted to address. I felt a sense of misgiving as I picked up my pen. I would be looking back at a time when I felt scared and alone, a time that was painful for me to remember.

My hand trembled as I put the pen to the paper. But when I started writing, I couldn't stop. The words poured out like an avalanche, along with the tears. I felt once again my loneliness at the loss of my parents, my anguish over the hurtful words that injured my tender spirit, and my pain at the physical abuse I received.

When the stream of words finally subsided, I sat and stared at the letter in amazement, trying to understand the reason for all that had happened, and feeling once again the misfortune of the situation in general. I had ignored the truth for twenty years, but it was there all the time, just stuffed away, its existence denied, its reality doubted.

I didn't sign my name to the letter—I never intended to mail it. I put it away in a drawer, thinking maybe I would share it later with my group at DAP. It wasn't until several days had passed that I began to feel troubled about it, not that I had written the letter, but that the problem was still unresolved. I had expressed my feelings, but I needed desperately to be confirmed in my interpretation of that experience. I wanted to hear my sister admit that it was true, to say she was sorry. I wanted her to explain why—somehow, some way—and to say that she loved me.

But from my sister's perspective, I had always been in the wrong. I had no real belief that she would try to see herself or any episode from my point of view. Somehow, it would all be my fault, while my sister would appear pious and charitable for having taken me in. I feared that she would respond in anger if I ever ventured to question her motives or behavior.

I began to consider confronting her, but I wasn't sure I dared. It would be frightening. We were both grown women, but the roles that had guided our relationship earlier in life still held power over me.

I took my predicament to DAP for a private session with Joanne. She put me through an exercise of imagining my sister there in the office with us. Then she had me read the letter aloud to my sister. As I proceeded, Joanne would interrupt me from time to time to inquire how she looked, what she was doing, how she was reacting. I could actually envision her sitting there across from me, her face red and galled, her hands wringing as she listened, exposed. I could hear her just as if she were there—saying it wasn't true, it was all lies, I was making it up. It was uncanny, it felt so real. When I finished, we discussed the possibility of asking her to come to DAP for a meeting. I knew that would be out of the question. But I was beginning to feel confident enough that I considered a plan in which I could confront her. I was still worried about her response, though. I could manage my part, but how would I feel if she denied it all?

With Joanne's reassuring confidence in me, I put my plan into action. I called and invited my sister to lunch. She seemed suspicious. To go out together would be a first for us, and I could tell she was uneasy with the suggestion. I had my doubts all along that she would co-operate. Nevertheless, after considerable hesitation, she agreed. But a few days later, she called and tried to cancel. I anticipated this and was prepared to meet her every excuse. In the end, a few days later, I faced my sister across a table at the Coachman's restaurant.

It was a quaint, older establishment with a composed atmosphere, attractively decorated. We were seated by the wall in a quiet section of the main dining room. It felt strange being alone with her for the first time in all those years. I couldn't remember ever going out with her alone before. She lit a cigarette and fidgeted a little as we waited for our waitress. After ordering our drinks, we talked casually for a while. The waitress brought our drinks and took our order. This gave me a little time to gather my courage. I could see her watching me, wondering why we were there. It couldn't be put off any longer. I had to take the risk of her failure to acknowledge the truth. If that was her response, at least she would have my testimony to live with even if she chose to deny it, and I would have finally spoken up for myself to her, challenging her hold over me.

I put down my drink and looked at her. "You may have heard that Chuck and I are having some problems we're trying to work out." I paused, and she looked at me questioningly. "We're involved in some counseling, and I've learned that I have some unresolved anger I need to deal with."

My sister's eyes shifted away from me, and she gave a little shrug as if to say, "So why are you telling me?"

I waited until her eyes met mine again, then pressed the point home. "That anger is with you." She started. I continued without giving her time to speak. "I've written you a letter about it, and I'd like you to read it right now."

Again, she winced, and tried to speak, but I interrupted. "Please, read it," I urged, pushing it into her hands.

After a moment, she nodded, and began to read.

I broke out in a cold sweat. I was amazed I had gotten this far, but I didn't know if I could take what was to come. I had fasted the day before, and I continued to pray, both for my sister and for myself as she read. I knew the letter by heart, and I recited the words to myself as she began:

> I am feeling a great deal of pain right now and some of the cause of that pain is the result of the way I was treated by you as I grew up.
>
> Because you used me as the brunt of your anger and took your feelings out on me, my feelings have been repressed and left unattended. You must have been angry about many things to be as mean as you were to me. Mother and Father divorcing, Mother working and your having to babysit us, Mother dying and your receiving the entire responsibility for raising us, your husband's lack of backbone and support in that task. Having to be strapped down with an old house, I could go on and on I'm sure.

At the end of this first page, where I had acknowledged her own frustrations, she paused and looked up at me, like she was surprised, remarking in amazement, "You're right—that's exactly how I felt."

I was locked in with her, waiting, as she continued to read.

> At any rate, I felt all your anger, both in your treatment of me and in the cruel, profane

113

things you said.

You showed me little mercy and little love or affection. My tears had almost no effect on you and you left me feeling hopeless, alone, hurting, unloved, uncared for, stupid, immature, useless, unimportant, ignorant, unwanted, used, unappreciated, no good, less than nothing. You put down any decision I made, you embarrassed me in front of my friends, you said ugly, untrue things about me to your friends, you criticized me for the way I did things, my grades, my sewing, my cooking, my work. You had very little good to say to me.

Couldn't you see the child in me? You killed her with your hate. You took away her spirit and life, her joy. Were you jealous? She tried so hard to please you, to be good and you just kept right on cutting away at her. The things you called me, the things you said, cut into my very heart over and over again until there was nothing left. You treated me worse than you would an animal and yet you never said, "I'm sorry." Why did you do these things to me? Didn't you know I was human, that I had a heart that could be wounded or broken by how you treated me? Did you have any feelings toward me at all? I tried to love you, to make you happy, to live peacefully with you and to get along, but sometimes there was nothing I could do. You chose to be mean and to take your feelings out on me.

By this time, her hands were shaking, and she looked very pale. "Please, go on. Finish the letter, please," I begged.

She read on:

You have wounded my spirit. You have left me

bleeding and dying and walked on by, on the other side of the road. And now I suffer with the pain of my life as a partial result of what you did to me. I am laying on you some of the responsibility for what and who I am today.

I am feeling anger and pain, and you are the cause for much of it. I have repressed it for years and now as it comes out, I feel hurt all over my body. How could you do it to me over and over again? How could you be so mean to me? How could you cut me so with your words? How could you hate me when I needed your love so much?

How do I feel about you now? I feel numb, like looking at the dead body of someone I love. Numb like not knowing what I feel because I hurt so much. Do I love you? I don't know. I know that I want to. I feel blocked away from you like you're standing with your hands raised up in front of you holding me back. It feels like you're insensitive to me, like I am an inanimate object. I feel like something that is there, that people look at and say "oh" like "so what?" and then they go on and nothing is different; nothing changes. It feels like you still don't care about me one way or the other. You could take me or leave me; you're indifferent to me. It leaves me feeling still worthless, unimportant, unwanted, unneeded, unloved. Why do I still care? Why do I still love you? I don't know! All I know is that I hurt, I hurt really bad and I'm very sad.

When she finally finished, she raised her head, but would not look at me. Her face was sallow. Her lips moved a little but there was no sound. She appeared devastated and scared. I waited, not knowing what was coming next, but less afraid of a tirade than before.

At last, she spoke. "It's all true, M'Liss. It's all true."

She lowered her eyes as she laid the letter down on the table. "You're right, and I'm sorry."

That was all. She didn't say anything else. I sat there speechless in shock at her admission. It wasn't much. It wasn't the response the letter deserved, but it was all I would get, and for now, it was enough. I had needed the confirmation of those experiences for all those years. Up until that moment, I was the only one who believed it ever happened. With her admission, my sister validated my feelings, fears, and experiences.

Never in all the times she had abused me verbally or physically had she ever said she was sorry or that she had been wrong. Now I heard them both. I wanted to get up and leave before anything happened that would take it away.

We dropped the subject immediately. I told her a little about Chuck and me, about our separation, and treatment. She was only mildly interested, and we moved to lighter conversation. Without lingering, we finished our lunch and left, both feeling anxious to be gone, but for different reasons.

In the days that followed my meeting with my sister, I repeated to myself several times the question I had asked her near the end of the letter, "Why do I still care?" Working with determination at DAP, to resolve this with myself, Joanne led me through a thorough self-analysis to help me realize how carefully I had been programmed. I judged myself as success or failure on the basis of how well I lived up to other people's rules and expectations. The "tapes" I had been given from the major influences in my life—my family and the church—were continuing to control my feelings, my self-evaluations and my self-worth.

My marriage was my identity. I held high ideals and expectations for it. My "tapes" required me to have breakfast on the table every morning, sex whether I wanted it or not, a clean house even if I had to pick up after everyone, and no nagging, criticizing, or complaining. If I was abused, there was something wrong with me; I didn't try hard enough, I wasn't good enough, my expectations were too high, I wasn't tolerant enough, I wasn't submissive like I was supposed to be. I used to feel guilty for taking a nap in the middle of the day. I wouldn't allow myself such a luxury because my "tapes" told me that was unproductive and selfish. I set myself up for failure. Yet I didn't expect others to live up to these standards. I was understanding and tolerant of their failures. But for myself, there was no excuse, there were no exceptions.

In looking at my parenting "tapes," I found that I took the responsibility of being a parent very seriously. I worked hard at doing a good job. I read a lot of books on the subject to improve my skills. I participated with and supported my children in almost all their activities. I worked at home so I would be there for them most of the time. Yet I discovered that I held stringent standards for what I expected, and as a result, I would get hooked by my "tapes" as a failure if I missed a school party, if I wasn't home when they needed me, or I neglected to read them their stories for even one night. If my children smoked, swore, sassed a teacher or rebelled in any way, I had labored in vain. If they didn't get good grades at school, I hadn't helped them enough. If they didn't get their work done at home or if they forgot a chore, I hadn't impressed on them their responsibilities. Push them to perfection, or suffer defeat. They had their share of "tapes" too, that I passed onto them, and for that I felt bankrupt, because by now, that was the last thing I wanted to do. All I worked for and believed in was backfiring in my face.

Chuck, too, had "tapes," just as devastating to him as mine were to me. His told him that if he didn't have a college education, he was worthless. If he wasn't rich, he was unsuccessful. If he was in the blue-collar working class, he was unimportant. To make a mistake or get lost was unforgivable. That meant he was stupid and incompetent. For me to disagree with him or to criticize him meant he was ignorant and foolish. We were two peas in a pod, only with different "tapes" feeding us discouragement and defeat. What a treadmill. It was time to get off, time to reevaluate and redefine our standards. We called it "changing our stinking thinking."

So I gave myself permission to make some mistakes. I interpreted Jesus' words, "Love your neighbor as yourself," in a new way for me and put myself first. I discovered that when my needs were taken care of, I was in a far better frame of mind to meet the needs of others. It was uncomfortable and scary at first. Would I become selfish, sloppy, or careless? Would I be too liberal? Yet it was time for the pendulum to start swinging in the other direction, it was too far to one side. What a relief to let go, to give myself room for mistakes, time to be sick, permission to just feel lazy and give into it, and then feel okay about it after. I was making some significant changes and feeling stronger and more comfortable with them. I was ready to tackle another painful issue, the church.

I had been dissatisfied with the congregation we belonged to for a number of years. And now with the battles I was engaged in, my church seemed irrelevant. We had been attending there for nine years and had been involved in a number of ways. We taught Sunday school together part of that time, and we were also active in a couples group and in a book study group. Plus, I had taught several Sunday classes myself as well as a ladies' morning Bible study class. Yet on the whole I felt unrelated. My church seemed segregated from my struggles, insulated from life, oblivious to reality. The sermons sounded like "pie in the sky," "save the world," yet I was dying. The God I was hearing about was only interested in people being saved. After that, you were on your own. It was like "being saved" solved everything else. That God wasn't big enough for what I was wrestling with. My impression was that no one there had any difficulties. They were all saints. I was the only oddball. If I had problems, I kept them to myself and pretended that everything was intact. I felt alone, like I was a freak, a leper. I stood apart. What I needed was to hear about the God who was interested in the smallest conflict, but who at the same time was great enough to handle the biggest.

There were several people from church who knew about Chuck's and my situation. They included several of the couples from our book group and the minister and his wife. Of these, only one person took the time to call and express love and support. She did this every week. Chuck never heard from anyone.

The minister knew I was dissatisfied, for I had been open in expressing it to him on many occasions. Then, after the betrayal of my friend, coupled with my general discontent with the church, I withdrew my membership and started going to another denomination. I needed to know the God who cared about my trials, the one who would love me with all my failings, the one who would give me room to grow, room to make mistakes without the fear of rejection or excommunication.

I told the minister I was leaving and going someplace else. In his response to me, he equated my leaving his denomination with "falling away" from Christ. After I left, I never heard from him or his wife again, not even as one human being concerned for the welfare and progress of another. His interest in us only went as far as getting us back to the church, and when he realized we did not intend to return, his concern ended.

When it became apparent to the rest of the congregation that we were gone, though they didn't know the cause or our present personal dilemma, their reaction was to ignore us. No one called to inquire "Where are you? We miss you," or, "Can we help you? We care." I felt a betrayal of a different kind. The "tapes" began to play again. This time, the messages I was hearing were "You're unwanted. We don't miss you. We don't need you. We don't care about you. We're glad you're not here." That may not have been what people there intended to say to us, but their indifference and lack of response to our leaving left us no other interpretation. That kind of Christianity, where the Christian "passes by on the other side," or is afraid of getting involved, I could do without. What was the church for? What was Christianity about? I knew that I would have to redefine it, or else I didn't need it. It was a good question, and in answering it, I gained freedom to break away from my unreasonable beliefs, my self-condemning tapes.

For me, Christianity has become an individual matter. It has nothing to do with what church I go to or what that church believes. It has to do with me and who I am, how I handle every opportunity and struggle of my day. I attend where I feel strengthened, so that when I leave, I feel girded up for the battle, challenged to meet every obstacle with the spirit of Christ. I ask for the right to go where I wish, without being condemned for what I believe is best for me. And I give that same right to others.

Through all of this reevaluation and redefining of my spirituality, I looked for my support to Domestic Abuse Project, to my dearest friend Nancy, to the one woman at church who continued to call, and to my middle sister Dorothy. All in all, it felt like a scrawny list after all I had done for others in the past.

CHAPTER 14

Chuck's move to the apartment seems in retrospect to be the turning point in this rehabilitation process. It was devastating for all of us. Nevertheless, it was necessary for the self-management experience and for the decision-making period Chuck needed to go through.

He went from not being responsible for much to being accountable for everything. The function of taking care of himself was the first requirement for which Chuck really had to put out effort. Certain things had to be done to maintain himself. These were things that had always been done for him.

It took Chuck several weeks to master the chore of fixing his breakfast and packing his lunch before making it to the bus for work. Usually he only managed one or the other, but rarely both. He learned gratitude for the years I had done it for him. He began to appreciate the variety of foods I had served him. Now, he had none. He ate the same thing for days on end.

Grocery shopping was another new experience for him. At first he bought what he liked, what looked tempting and appetizing. But soon he found his money was going too quickly and his food wasn't going far enough. So he learned to watch for sales—dented cans, day old bread, etc.

Cleaning his apartment was another challenge. He was used to me picking up after him. Now he found his things lying around everywhere in disorder and confusion. He couldn't believe how quickly it got messy. He soon realized what an ongoing drudgery of deliberate concentrated effort it took to keep things put away.

With his laundry, he experienced the same thing. It seemed anything he settled on to wear was in the wash. It felt like he no sooner had the laundry done and he was out of clothes again. He found it to be a time-consuming nuisance.

He was forced to take care of himself by confronting his neighbors about their noise and loud music. For a number of days, he would complain to me about it. When I didn't take care of it for him, he was obliged to take the matter into his own hands. Having to go to his neighbors and voice his complaint was very disconcerting to him. He felt powerless and awkward. But he did it, not just once, or to just one neighbor, but many times and to several different people over the four months he lived there.

When Chuck first moved into his apartment, he expected the children to just drop by and visit him. When they didn't, he became depressed and very angry. He demanded to know why I wasn't sending them up to see him. I informed him that if he wanted a relationship with his children he would have to develop it. They were busy with other things and their own active schedules. They didn't think much about him. In the past, I would beg him to spend time with them or to read to them, but he would refuse. Now, he was ready to do that. So he began to call them from work and make plans with each one of them. They responded willingly and gladly. They would go out to eat with him, or he would cook their supper. Sometimes they would stay the night in his apartment. If he had to go to work the next day, he would fix their breakfast and then they would ride their bikes home when he left for work.

With such willingness and cooperation from all of them, their relationship began to build.

Chuck's discomfort in unknown situations and his need to blame someone for his problems was another area in which being on his own forced him to acknowledge responsibility. One evening he went to Minneapolis to look into a new self-help group that was starting up there. He got confused with his directions and became lost downtown. He was frantic. He ran around like a chicken with its head cut off, first in one direction, then in another, with no rhyme or reason governing his steps. Finally he went up to a policeman and asked for help. By this time, he was so upset that the policeman backed away from him and suggested he go across the street to a bar for a drink and calm down. With no one to blame for his predicament but himself, he was faced with the stark reality of his own falliblity.

When he had time on his hands and no one to do anything with, he was faced with his own need for friends and activities.

Another objective accomplished during Chuck's stay in the apartment was the rebuilding of his relationship with his mother. She had been aware of our problem and decided to visit us. Usually when she came, we were all together with little chance for serious conversation. This time she and Chuck were on their own, and the results were beautiful to watch. Chuck came to the house to pick her up and they spent the evening together. He took her to a restaurant near his apartment. There he began talking with her, sharing a letter he had written which chronicled all the incidents of violence and all the years of pain and anger he had endured. She listened and considered her part in the abuse and talked openly with him about it. Afterwards, they went back to his apartment and continued to talk until the early hours of the morning. They reviewed many of his memories and events of the past. He had replaced his bed with two twin size foam mattresses that were piled on top of each other on the floor. Whenever he had company for the night, such as his children, he laid the mattresses side by side like twin beds. In this way he could easily accommodate a guest. This is how he and his mother lay and talked. She shared with him how painful it was for her to see him living like that. She was anxious to see him get his life back together and be home with his family. In the morning he got up and made breakfast for her. She had a difficult time just sitting there allowing him to serve her. She wanted to make the bed, do some of the cooking, or set the table, something to help. But Chuck insisted, assuring her that he wanted to learn to take care of himself and acknowledging to her his belief in the value of it. As they continued to converse together, a new door began opening for them, to a new relationship which they now had the opportunity to build, a relationship of care, trust, understanding, and forgiveness. At the same time, the door was being closed to past resentments, hurts, bitterness, misunderstandings, and anger.

While Chuck's mother was at our house, I was able to spend several nights with him in his apartment. This experience helped dispel my misgivings. He shared with me how much he was learning and how badly he felt that he never had a real appreciation for all I had done for him in the past. His appreciation was genuine and his understanding of the difficulties was real. He was coming from an entirely different perspective. As Chuck's confidence in himself increased, and as he took responsibility for himself and his actions, and as I grew stronger in my resolve to stay out of his issues and learned not to rescue or take care of him, we began to discuss his coming home.

So, one evening shortly before his mother was to return to her home in Missouri, I stayed the night at his apartment and we sat down and drew up a list of expectations and goals for his return. We alloted a scheduled time for him to take one of the children out each Saturday. He agreed to make his own breakfast and lunch each day, to help with the preparations for company and in the cleanup after they left. We would have a family conference each Sunday evening to air problems and schedule activities. We set aside specific time on a regular basis to talk without interruptions, to keep issues cleared up so they couldn't accumulate as in the past. Every other Thursday one of us would have the night off to go out with a friend. It was to be a free night to allow Chuck a specific time that he could count on to maintain his male acquaintances. This is considered essential for men who batter.

One thing was clear to me as we negotiated our terms. Chuck was committed and determined to share in the responsibilities of maintaining his family. When I noted to him my observations, he told me that being alone in his apartment had given him a lot of time to think. The possibility of losing his family and the reality of how much we meant to him was the most valuable lesson of the whole experience. Where he had vacillated in the past between staying and leaving, between caring and "not giving a damn," he now had no reservations. He wanted more than anything, at all costs, to be part of his family. So we worked out our terms and went over them together with our counselors at DAP, and Chuck moved back home.

The apartment had served its purpose. It held warm precious memories for me of the nights I had stayed there with Chuck, but it reminded him of the pain and suffering he had been through. Yet we laugh sometimes when we think about it, wondering what his neighbors must have thought about the strange parade of guests he entertained.

However, our work wasn't finished. We still needed

training in our communication skills. We required new methods for disciplining the children, and we needed guidance in redeveloping our trust for each other. These issues would take many months of work to get through, and we would still need a lot of help and instruction. But we were on our way, with the biggest struggles behind us.

With Chuck back home, new challenges confronted us. One was the adjustment for me of letting go of the things I had managed in the past that Chuck was now doing himself. Another was getting our children to accept his participation in the direction and discipline of their lives.

The relationships Chuck began building with our children while he was in the apartment have been maintained. When he goes out each week with one of them, he takes along a list of topics or issues he wants to discuss. He adds to his list each week and he encourages them to contribute to it things they would like to talk about. Whenever a discipline problem arises, Chuck is informed and involved in working out the solution. His commitment to his children is also reflected in the time he now takes for night classes in parenting skills. He wants to be a part of his family, he chooses to be involved.

When Chuck returned home, years of neglected household repairs awaited him. Over that long period of time, he had with indignation and irritation made only those repairs that were absolutely necessary. The little unimportant things were left undone. Chuck, determined to change, sat down and made an inventory of all the jobs he needed to bring up to date. He invited me to add anything to it that he had overlooked. Then he went to work, and week by week he whittled down the list, one task at a time. Two positive things resulted from his efforts: one, he felt better about himself, and two, he relieved himself of the guilt of neglected responsibilities. They were things he knew he should do, and as long as they were left undone, they had a subtle way of digging at his conscience and at his self-esteem. Now, if something needs fixing, I call it to his attention, and he takes care of it first chance he has. He has accepted this as part of his contribution to his family's well-being.

One of the larger tasks Chuck took on was the management of our finances. I had handled the deposit and paid the bills for twenty years. Whenever Chuck wanted to make an expensive purchase, he would look to me for an evaluation of our financial condition and a judgment as to whether or not we could handle it. If I said we couldn't afford the item, he would hold me liable as the cause. He would harbor animosity against me, resenting and blaming me that we didn't have the money he needed. Now, he is responsible for the dispensing of our funds. If he wants to make a costly investment, he decides for himself if he can afford it. This has taken a tremendous burden off of my shoulders and it has broadened his to carry it.

Another area where Chuck has made significant change is in picking up after himself. I used to pick up his dirty clothes every morning after he left for work. And I would hang up the clean ones he left lying around. All that has changed. He now leaves a spotless room every day. This disposition has carried over into the way he now maintains his garage. His workshop was in constant chaos. His tools were usually scattered around and he was always missing one thing or another. When he would work on a project in the house, the mess was left for me to clean up. Now he maintains a clean, orderly workbench and any messes he makes, he cleans up himself when he is through.

Chuck had a number of "tapes" that needed reprogramming just as I did. They controlled the way he reacted when he was late, or when he was lost, or when

I would ask him to pick up something from the store or run some errand. When he was lost, his tapes told him he was irresponsible and inadequate. Now, the minute he is unsure of his directions, he stops and asks for help. His tape for being late labeled him disrespectful and undependable. He would drive like a mad man, yelling at me for taking so long to get ready. He would never help dress the children or lend a hand to pack the picnic, or assist in locking the doors. He would just wait in the car and then criticize and blame me for our tardiness. Now he helps me get ready if I have special preparations to make. And, if we're late, we're late, he can let go of it and still be okay. The tapes for running errands characterized him as a hen-pecked messenger boy. But, his attitude now is one of willing, cheerful, cooperation, glad to be of help.

He has also given himself permission to return items to the store when he is dissatisfied with a purchase. In the past, he would be angry and resentful if he found his purchase defective or of poor quality. He would keep the item and then curse it when it failed to function the way he expected it to. Now if he is dissatisfied, he returns the item and complains to the source—someone who can do something about it, instead of to me.

Shortly after Chuck returned home, he had the opportunity to resolve his feelings of anger with his dad. His parents divorced a few years after Chuck and I were married. We heard from his dad a couple times a year. He came to see us twice in twenty years and called just a few times more. His dad had heard we were having problems and called one evening to see how we were doing. Chuck, feeling safer confronting his dad at a distance, took the letter he had written at DAP and read it to him over the phone. He shared his hatred because of the dog incident, his disrespect because of the savage spankings, his resentment over the constant criticism, and his rebellion, anger and frustration with the futility of trying to please. Chuck laid it all out, yelling with pain, swearing in anger. His dad listened and acknowledged the injustice of what he had done. He shared with Chuck that he had thought of many of those incidents with regret and discontent. He was sorry and if he had it to do over, he'd do some things very differently. They made peace. A few months later, his dad flew up for a visit. Though they never discussed the phone conversation, they talked freely, building a new relationship much like he had done with his mother.

None of these changes or confrontations were easy. They didn't just happen. They came by the vehicle of pain, sweat and tears. They came about through the conscious resolution that Chuck made to take responsibility for himself, to make peace with his parents, to save his marriage and to keep his family. They came at a high price, the sacrifice of himself. He had to lose his life in order to find it.

CHAPTER 15

Because domestic violence affects the behavior of the entire family, our children would need help too. They would need guidance in interpreting the effect the violence had on them as well as affirmation and reassurance in adjusting to the changes we were making. When we approached them about their going to DAP, we were met with opposition. It was okay for Mom and Dad, but another story when it came to their being involved. After some persuasion, they relented and complied.

I made innumerable trips back and forth to DAP.

Elgin was to be in a pre-adolescent group, and the girls would be together in the teen group. Though Elgin was in a separate group, the procedures, exercises, and goals were the same. They began each week checking in with a weather report to express how they were feeling that day: sunny-happy, partly cloudy-mediocre, cloudy-sad, and stormy-angry. After check in, they might draw pictures, play a game, have a discussion, or a presentation, or work on personal issues.

One week they drew pictures of themselves and how they looked when they were angry. Another week, they drew one of how they saw their family.

One of the games they played was to have a "scared feeling" word pinned to their back, and then they had to guess the word while the others helped them by acting it out.

They worked together in group to analyze their definition of male and female roles. Next, they redefined both roles in a way that felt comfortable for each individual there.

They reviewed the cycle of violence, as Chuck and I had done, and looked at it in relation to themselves and their conduct. They examined their own behavior during the cycle and discovered for themselves that, when Chuck's temper was escalating, they would check with him from time to time to see how he was feeling. Sometimes, they would take care of him, or try to avoid or humor him. Other times, they would act up more, trying to draw fire off me. During the explosion phase, they would sometimes start fighting among themselves, they would turn up the volume on the T.V., sometimes leave if they could, or tune themselves out. And, in the honeymoon phase, they would take advantage of their dad's guilt by asking if they could stay up late, or if he would take them somewhere they wanted to go, or buy them something they wanted. They learned that the results of taking advantage of Chuck's shame produced feelings of guilt in themselves. Or, they would try to take care of his guilt by reaffirming him, offering to help him with some task, or by doing something special for him.

They discussed with their groups the effects of the abuse and what the violence taught them. The messages they got were many: they were not okay, they were sometimes responsible for the violence, it was okay to hit. They learned not to trust others, because they had heard "I'm sorry" before. They learned to manipulate because it wasn't always safe to be direct. They learned to deny the violence, it was the family's secret.

They shared together, expressing and discussing their

long suppressed feelings. They listed their feelings: ashamed, depressed, helpless, guilty, fearful, angry, revengeful, rebellious, hateful, confused. They examined their own maneuvering, how they tried to confuse and distract the escalation process. They found they used different means such as underachieving at school, running away from home, shutting down under the guise of "they can't hurt me any more," or care-taking to delay the explosion. They also made drawings of their anger and they discussed "Whose fault is it?" They were taught how to set limits and boundaries for themselves. And they each made their own protection plan. With their groups, they shared their grief and sadness, working through it with support from one another. It was a healthy process and I was grateful that my children were cooperative and had the opportunity to be a part of it.

The girls completed their twelve weeks of teen group, and their therapist suggested they repeat the sessions in separate groups. She believed their participation had been limited the first time through, possibly because each was intimidated by the presence of the other.

So I hit the road again, first with Rebecca for twelve weeks, and then with Rachel for twenty-four. Rachel enjoyed her second round so much she wanted a third. I believe I wore a groove in the road all the way over there and back. Nevertheless, I was willing to run my tail off, if that's what it took for them to have that advantage.

With our children, we experienced countless gains and setbacks. It seemed like for every two steps forward, we'd go back one. When Chuck was in the apartment, all three children misbehaved in different ways, and I needed help in resolving my issues with them. I had to take some time for some private sessions with Elgin and his therapist and Rachel and hers.

Elgin was getting into other people's things in the house, lying, breaking rules, not being where he said he was going. My trust in him was leveled and I felt powerless, unable to deal with it. My fears were devastating and I was overreacting. I believed the worst: he was a delinquent at age ten. Afraid he was really going to mess himself up, I was ready to put him into a foster home. Feeling incompetent, I sought help from his counselor. We headed for DAP and I began to wish I had a dollar for every trip. The therapist there helped Elgin to understand what his behavior was doing to me. And she helped me to realize that my projections of Elgin's future were unrealistic in proportion to what he was presently doing. I relaxed a little.

Then after a few days, Elgin started in again testing the limits. So it was back to DAP! I was discouraged and wrung out. It seemed every time I turned my back, he was doing something he knew he wasn't supposed to do. This time, he was lighting matches in the house. This was against the rules. He had found some wet fire crackers, and he was trying to dry them out using the matches to build a fire under them in the oven. I panicked, envisioning him as an arsonist and willfully rebellious and defiant. So we found ourselves in another session, working again on the issue of his untrustworthiness and my irrational conclusions.

Then, there were the private conferences for Rachel. Her therapist had brought a specific problem to my attention. Rachel had shared with her group that she had been vomiting her food in an effort to lose weight, and her counselor was concerned. She felt that Rachel had an eating disorder and wanted us to be aware of her behavior.

The next issue that brought us to DAP was shoplifting. Rachel had been caught in a local department store stealing makeup, and I was alarmed. Rachel was a kleptomaniac. She was going to have a police record. My imagination was running away with me and the trust between us was fragmented.

In the meantime, Rachel and Elgin wanted to quit their cello lessons. They both had played for more than four years and neither one had been very enthusiastic after the first month. With Chuck gone, I had no energy left to battle with them about their practice, so the best recourse seemed to be to give in. They were elated. I did hold my ground with their piano, though there was some resistance there too. My belief in the benefit of musical knowledge was intense enough to fortify me against total defeat by their objections.

Rebecca's rebellion took on a different form. Her reaction to our family meetings was resistance and uncooperativeness. Her response to treatment was antagonism. The clash came with her denial of the violence: "I never saw it happen." Then she relinquished a little and moved into minimizing it: "It wasn't that bad. You're making a big deal out of nothing." And finally, she completely refused to talk about it. She tried to emotionally detach herself from the family and all we were doing. She was "Daddy's girl," and to acknowledge the abuse was the same as exposing and betraying him. She had taken on our shame, our degradation, and even though we had exposed it ourselves and admitted our charade, she would not accept it. She was ashamed of us. We were a scandal, an embarrassment to her. We had taught her well to guard the family secret. Her mutiny was to resist the changes we were making and to deny the problem.

The children's misbehavior wasn't all bad, even though it was stressful for us. It was a sign we were all getting better. In the past, they wouldn't have risked doing some of the things they were trying for fear of the possible consequences. Even after Chuck returned home, the insurrections continued.

Rachel had a friend over one night to go to the neighborhood theater for the late movie. I was to pick them up after the show. I went to bed, and set the alarm for eleven to go and get them.

Half asleep, I drove to the theater. They were giggling and clowning around in front when I arrived. They lightheartedly climbed into the back seat of the car, their capering persisting as I started for home. After driving several blocks, I detected the faint smell of alcohol in the car. I drove a little further, wondering how to confront them. Finally, I said, "Where did you get the liquor?"

A unamious chorus rose from the back seat, "We haven't been drinking."

I repeated the question just as before and again received innocent denial. Exasperated, I replied, "This car smells like a brewery, and I haven't been drinking, so who has?"

Again, indifferent dissent. I felt defeated and ineffectual. The law had helped me before, perhaps it would again. I turned the car around and announced, "Okay, if you won't tell me, I am taking you down to the police station, Rachel, to have your blood checked for alcoholic content."

I had her immediate attention. She quickly told me some boys in the theater had some beer and they each had a sip.

I panicked. "Rachel, how do you know there wasn't something more in there?"

"Oh, Mother," she responded with a sound of offended indignation in her voice, "the cans were unopened."

I was being lied to, the story was changing too fast. "I don't know what to believe, so we'll just let the police test settle the question."

"Mother," she cried, her tone changing to contempt, "we each had a can and drank about half. That's all.

That's the honest truth."

It was too late. Not knowing what to believe, I would not yield. I arrived at the station and with me leading the way, they followed behind like cowering sheep. Walking up to the clerk, I explained the situation and requested a blood test for my daughter.

He cocked his head and gave me a blank puzzled stare. I repeated my statement with more determination in my voice, and he seemed to get the picture. Telling us to have a seat, he called for someone from juvenile. When the officer arrived, I explained the situation. He looked shocked at my request. "That's a very expensive test," he stated, then continued, "and since it's Saturday night, all our machines are out." He suggested we go to another room to talk privately. When we were by ourselves, I indicated that I understood his situation in regard to the blood test. I went on to admit that my objective more than anything was to frighten Rachel so that she would think twice before drinking again. He appeared supportive, reassuring me that he thought I had already accomplished my goal. He went on to suggest that when we returned to the lobby where the girls were waiting, he would tell me in front of them that if I had any further trouble, to give him a call.

With that, the girls and I returned to the car. The drive home was quiet. When we pulled into the garage and got out of the car, I told Rachel's friend that I didn't think it would be necessary for me to tell her folks about the drinking. She started crying, "Oh, Mrs. Switzer thank you. It won't happen again, I promise, I promise." Rachel, looking shaken, apologized too.

We all hugged, there were more tears and promises to be good, then we all went in to bed.

With Elgin, one of the gains we enjoyed was his willingness to own up sooner whenever he was caught doing something wrong. In the past, he would deny everything, no matter how conclusive the evidence was.

One day, he arrived home from school about half an hour late. In the meantime, I had received a call from one of his classmates asking if Elgin had her brother's walkie talkies. They had been left on the bus by mistake. When Elgin came in, I questioned him. He said the bus was late, and, no, he didn't have the walkie talkies.

Two days later, I received a call before school, this time from the boy's mother, asking again about the walkie talkies. I let her talk to Elgin saying I would listen on the extension. She told him one of the kids saw him the day before with the antenna from one of the walkie talkies and she wanted to know how he happened to have it. He told her he found the antenna on the bus. She was suspicious. She recounted that when her son got off the bus, there were only three students left to be dropped off. Her daughter had called Elgin and one other student. Neither of them had it. The third student didn't have a phone and she herself had driven to his home to inquire. She had also gone to the bus company and checked the bus. Therefore, since he had the antenna, she was skeptical about his denial.

He denied it again. With that, she sounded baffled, discouraged, like she was going to let the matter drop. But I wasn't satisfied that the investigation was complete. I questioned Elgin further, and his answers sounded shaky. With that, the woman reflected, "I was going to let the matter go, but upon reconsideration, I think I will take it to the principal. The walkie talkies were brand new and my son had taken them to school for show and tell."

Upon hearing this, Elgin put down his phone and came running into the room where I was and asked me if I would hold the line for a moment. I paused and he told me he had taken the walkie talkies. The night he was late coming from the bus, he and his friend had been playing with them and they had broken the antenna. I told him he would have to explain it to the mother on the phone. He backed away, shaking his head. I urged him on, saying, "You took the responsibility for those walkie talkies when you removed them from the bus. Now you need to follow through with it by admitting what has happened."

So he went back to his phone and repeated the story to her. When he finished, she responded, "Elgin, I really appreciate your owning up to taking them. It took a great deal of courage to do that, and it will save a lot of people trouble and embarrassment. You will have to pay for the one you broke and then we'll drop the matter."

He agreed and we hung up the phone. Then he came back into the room where I was and apologized for what he had done. It felt good to see him acknowledging his wrongs, and the woman's positive response to his confession was reinforcing. He had taken a risk and survived.

Meanwhile, at DAP, we started family group. Other than ours, there were three other families involved. This came to a total of twelve children, ages two to sixteen, nine adults, and two counselors. What a zoo. You wouldn't think anything could be accomplished with such a diverse crowd. There was never a dull moment, and there were many distractions, but the benefit of the group experience justified any inconvenience. Sometimes we would break into our own family groups to discuss specific assignments: "What was the violence like?" "How did it affect each member in the family?" After sharing our answers with our own family, we would come together as a group and relate what we heard or shared, and how we felt about it. It was unendurably painful for the men, as they listened to how their behavior had affected their wives and children. Yet, as each shared their hurts, the pain brought healing. The whole experience had Rebecca in tears. She didn't like talking about it at all and wanted us to forget it happened and go on with life. The anguish for her was in seeing her father exposed and feeling his shame. She wanted to keep it hidden as we had always done, but in the face of so much openness in the group, she was breaking down, her defenses crumbling.

Rachel revealed that when her dad was violent, she wanted to beat him up, somehow get back at him so he would know how it felt. She believed that once he knew, he wouldn't do it again.

Elgin talked about how terrified he felt, and how he wanted to leave or somehow shut it out.

Chuck, listening to how we were each affected, started crying. He had looked at it before, but hearing it again all at once overwhelmed him. The enormity of the load was hard to bear. And he was carrying it all alone. He shared with the group that part of the burden belonged to his past, his parents and grandparents. He wasn't trying to deny his own intent to be abusive. He had accepted the responsibility for that months ago. But in acknowledging that the origin of that behavior went back several generations, he felt alone in doing something about it. The generations before had left the burden for him. By opening up his sad lonely feelings to his children he gave them the opportunity to share his pain. They reached back to him with forgiveness and reaffirming support.

One of the more fun things we did in family group was role play. On one occasion, the children took the part of the parents and the parents became the children. It helped give each of us a better perspective of the other's viewpoint on a given issue. It was amazing how insightful and creative the children were in exploring ways of resolving conflicts.

We played games in family group too. Elgin's favorite was one where we got together in a small, tightly-formed circle and then everyone reached across and took the hand of two different people. When that was executed as instructed, we ended up with a large tangled knot of people. The object then was to untangle ourselves without letting go. We all had to cooperate with one another to do this. We had to listen and obey as well as instruct each other. Sometimes it couldn't be completely undone, but when we were successful, we finished with a full circle of satisfied participants. The game demonstrated the importance of every member, the necessity for everyone's cooperation, and the reality that not all problems are solvable.

Family group therapy lasted for six weeks. We had become intimately acquainted with each other and when it was over, there were feelings of sadness and loss as we parted company.

We next went as a family for private sessions. We worked on our own family issues that weren't addressed in group. We were given the opportunity to practice under supervision some of the parenting and communication skills we had learned. The biggest issue we dealt with was our trust for one another. At first we all agreed that we trusted each other and had no reservations about it. But upon closer examination, the truth revealed that we each had different qualifications for how we trusted each other. I trusted Rebecca in a different way than I trusted Rachel. And my trust for Rachel was different from my trust of Elgin. As for my trust of Chuck, it was limited, and many areas still needed to be worked out. Our counselors taught us how to handle different encounters where trust was questionable or had been broken. They showed us the importance of sharing with the one who had violated our confidence how we felt about it, and then the necessity of stating clearly what we needed.

Another obstacle we dealt with in our family session was the subject of blame. Over the years, we had each learned it wasn't safe to make a mistake, or do something wrong. To survive, we improvised the "blame game" to pass the buck, to get the heat off ourselves. It was interesting to notice how we could come into a session with an issue against someone, and in record-breaking time, that person would have the subject off of himself or herself and onto someone else. Oftentimes the one who brought the issue up would soon find himself or herself on the hot spot and then he or she would scratch his or her head in curious amazement, wondering how he or she got there. We could throw blame back and forth like a red hot potato. We learned that as a result of the "blame game," nothing was ever resolved.

We worked together for about six months in these family sessions. As the counselor noted our progress and our ability to use our new skills more and more, the time had arrived for him to cut us loose. It was scary. We were like babies in the womb, secure, comfortable and protected as we grew and developed. We had used these family sessions for a safe place to present our tough issues to one another. We were used to the help of a third party. Could we now manage it ourselves? We were skeptical. We didn't want to let go. But in spite of our resistance, we were launched off, the umbilical cord cut.

EPILOGUE

According to statistics, our family won't make it. The chance of lasting change in abusive situations that have been going on for as long as ours is practically zero. Freedom from violence for our family cannot be guaranteed. It can only be sought after with dedicated determination. Our struggle isn't over just because we have completed two years of therapy. Like everyone else, we still have challenges with our children, struggles with health problems, bills to pay, decisions to make. What therapy did was to give us the tools for these challenges. But like athletes training for a race, we must continually exercise and practice to guard against the old behavior patterns that try to creep back into our lives. So in order to help keep alert, we have become involved helping others who suffer from and with abuse.

A year after our "graduation" from DAP, Chuck and I returned to take a course that trained us to facilitate self-help groups. Chuck works as a volunteer facilitator in charge of a Men's Self-Help Group that meets once a week. I'm working in a similar fashion with a battered women's group. Another way we remind ourselves of all we've been taught is by sharing our story as public speakers. We've made presentations at Advocate Training Sessions, for the United Way in their annual fundraising drive, and at DAP where we have shared with others there in treatment. This is our maintenance program. It benefits us as much as it helps others.

Yet there is another reason we are willing to expose ourselves and to share our story. We want to take part in eradicating the disease. Countless others have paved the way. They have labored without reward or recognition to get laws changed, and to establish shelters and safe houses. Many have studied and researched, gathering information and statistics. Institutions like Domestic Abuse Project are being established. Workshops to train and educate police and judges are being held. Because of these efforts, we have been helped. We want to join the ranks of those who are working to stop domestic violence.

Our family has received special attention because of our success in overcoming violence. It's unusual for a family to be able to make this kind of change and still remain together. So a great deal of recognition and praise has come our way. This gives us a chance to speak out. For example, we appeared on Minnesota Public Television, KTCA's production of *Turning Point*. The presentation was entitled *Battered Dreams* and focused on domestic violence and mandatory arrest for batterers. We shared some of our history and how the law had affected our situation. Sometime later, we participated in a similar presentation on ABC-TV. Ted Koppel interviewed us on *Nightline News,* giving domestic violence it's first national coverage. The University of Minnesota School of Journalism chose the subject of domestic violence for their journalistic magazine production. Entitled *A Silence Too Loud,* the magazine covered the entire spectrum of abuse through various stories and interviews. Our story was one of the feature articles entitled "Till Death Do Us Part."

And so we accepted the invitation to go public with our story, hoping to speed up the process of stopping domestic violence. We believe we have something to say to people to help them understand the problem and to acquaint them with available resources and assistance.

As a result of the publicity our story has attracted, some positive things have happened. Not only has it helped to inform the public and to change some laws, but our children have taken on a sense of pride in us. Instead of feeling the shame and embarrassment of our past, they have turned their focus to our achievements. And they have become more open themselves in talking about abuse.

But self-exposure comes with many price tags. Change isn't free or easy. And so some negative things have resulted as well. From both Chuck's and my families of origin have come complaints, threats, and abuse. They feel vulnerable to exposure by our openness. They would like to see us silenced. They would like to keep the secret hidden. Like them, Chuck and I feel guilty and ashamed of the past. Nevertheless, someone, somewhere, at some point in time must speak out to stop the abuse. Our changes have threatened many people. They have challenged the beliefs of some and have caused us to leave our church. They have exposed the wrongs of others and caused us to be rejected by some of the members of our families. They have challenged the commitment of others and cost us the loss of some friends. Yet paying this price is nothing to what we have gained. We have a family free of violence, new insights and spiritual beliefs based on our own experience and study, friends who are closer to us than our own families, and the joy and privilege of helping others who want to change.

I would like to be able to end this narration with "and they lived happily ever after." But that would not be accurate or realistic in the face of the daily conflicts of life. Our problem is not extinct. Like a dormant volcano, it could erupt unanticipated. If that happens, does it mean we have failed? We don't think so. Failure takes place when we quit, when we give up, when we walk away. We have a responsibility to ourselves and to each other to continue to participate in those things that stimulate us in the direction of our goal. Should there ever be a moment of violence again in our marriage, it will serve as a warning, not that we've failed, but that we've become complacent and indifferent, or overconfident and highminded. We'll need the humility of spirit to examine ourselves and the determination of heart to get up and try again. May God grant us patience with each other as we grow and as we fail. May we have humility to remember where we've been, how we got to where we are now, and how much further we still need to go. And most of all, grace to forgive those who have failed us and love to forgive ourselves.